The *Really* Fun Family Haggadah

This Haggadah was designed to achieve the original intent as explained in the Torah: To "tell your children" the story of Passover. Just as the section on the Four Children teaches us to appeal to children in a variety of ways, this Haggadah features:

- Meaningful explanations of the traditions
- Easy-to-read versions of the Passover story
- Fun facts and questions

Careful: Some questions have 2 or 3 answers!

Hopefully, these features will add meaning to your Seder and infuse both parents and children alike with a greater appreciation for the *ruach* (spirit), drama and joy of Passover.

Enjoy the fun facts and questions, they can keep your Seder fresh and entertaining from year to year. Try some one year, others the next. **Check your answers on pages 46-47** — that's fun too!

Chag Samei'ach,

Larry Stein   *Leah Sos*

The "Matzah Version" — a shorter Seder.
For those who absolutely need to conduct a brief service, we have placed a matzah icon and blue shading to note the Seder's essential steps and guide you through a 30-minute service prior to the meal. It's shorter than we would like, but still brings you through the essential steps of the Seder.

See the "Matzah Version" guide on page 3.

We do not recommend hurried Seders.
Part of the freedom we celebrate today on Passover is the ability to have a leisurely Seder. So, don't zip through the Seder to get to the food. Enjoy this time with family and friends, and delve deep into the meanings of Passover.

Questions... questions... questions.
Passover is a time to ask questions. The rabbis filled the Seder with unusual rituals and symbols to spark questions, even from children too young to read. Ask questions, it's an expression of our freedom. As slaves, we couldn't ask questions. Now, we can.

Look out for the nuts!
The Talmud says the Seder leader should give nuts to children to keep them awake during the service. My great grandfather used nuts for another purpose — to quiet people who were talking! If he became annoyed with your talking, he would throw nuts at you from across the table! Ouch!

The Seder's 14 Steps

Seder means "order." The rabbis first gave order to the Passover service more than 2,000 years ago by creating the Haggadah. While all Haggadot may look different, they all contain the same steps to fulfill the Seder's requirements.

Some families chant the 14 steps prior to the Seder. The 14 steps are marked throughout this Haggadah to make it easy for you to follow.
(Note: some Haggadot use 15 steps, splitting Motzi Matzah into two steps, Motzi and Matzah)

1. **Kadesh**
   קַדֵּשׁ
   Chant the *Kiddush* for the first cup of wine.

2. **Urchatz**
   וּרְחַץ
   Wash your hands.

3. **Karpas**
   כַּרְפַּס
   Recite the blessing and eat a vegetable dipped in salt water.

4. **Yachatz**
   יַחַץ
   Break the middle matzah and hide the larger half for the *Afikoman*.

5. **Maggid**
   מַגִּיד
   Tell the Passover story.

6. **Rochtzah**
   רָחְצָה
   Wash your hands and recite the blessing.

7. **Motzi Matzah**
   מוֹצִיא מַצָּה
   Recite the two blessings and eat the matzah.

8. **Maror**
   מָרוֹר
   Recite the blessing and eat the bitter herbs.

9. **Korech**
   כּוֹרֵךְ
   Eat the matzah and maror together (the Hillel Sandwich).

10. **Shulchan Orech**
    שֻׁלְחָן עוֹרֵךְ
    Serve the Festival meal.

11. **Tzafun**
    צָפוּן
    Eat the *Afikoman*.

12. **Barech**
    בָּרֵךְ
    Blessings After the Meal.

13. **Hallel**
    הַלֵּל
    Chant the *Hallel*.

14. **Nirtzah**
    נִרְצָה
    Acceptance: The conclusion of the Seder.

The Haggadah looks back into our past, then into our future.
The Haggadah is separated into two parts. Before the meal, the Haggadah looks back into our past, remembering how God helped us gain our freedom. After the meal, we look to our future: eating the Afikoman, singing about Elijah, chanting Hallel and concluding with, "Next year in Jerusalem!"

Before the invention of the printing press in the 1400s, very few Jews had a Haggadah. To help Jews remember the 14 steps of the Seder, the rabbis:
a) Put it on the Internet: www.14steps.com.
b) Produced catchy TV commercials.
c) Engraved the 14 steps on stone tablets.
d) Created a clever rhyme.

Enjoying Your Seder

The key to a great Seder:
      Get everyone involved!
That's the key to a great Seder — get everyone to participate with *ruach* (spirit). Children too young to read should be encouraged to sing or act out certain parts. And everyone should ask questions, lots of questions. The Seder leader should be part rabbi and part cheerleader. Everyone should get involved and appreciate the meaning of Passover.

Choosing what to do... what not to do.
Although you should consider your guest list in determining the content of your Seder, we believe it's important to do all 14 steps of the traditional Seder. If time is a major consideration, you may choose to shorten a few of the steps, and we've done that in some instances for you. For example, we offer a very brief children's version of the Passover story on page 16 as an alternative to a more complete version on page 19.

Try some of the extras, but not all of them.
We've added a lot of fun questions (in blue type) and explanations (in gray type) to spice up your Seder and deepen its meaning. But don't try to do all of them in one night — it's too much. Choose some this year, do others the next. If there's a lull in the action, fill in the time with some of the multiple-choice questions. Or, better yet, ask some questions of your own.

Check our checklist before you start.
The rear inside cover has a transliteration guide and a very helpful list of essentials you will need for your Seder. If you haven't led a Seder before, prepare ahead of time — it's a big endeavor, but well worth the effort. Enjoy!

Whatever you do:

Don't hurry — we did that enough as slaves.

Make every Seder special!

The "Matzah Version"
(30-minute service before the meal)
If time is truly a consideration, the Matzah version will take you through the essential steps (noted in Hebrew below) and some other key parts. This should take about 30 minutes before the meal, enabling you to enjoy a reasonably full service in a modest amount of time.

 If you choose this alternative, look for the Matzah icon and blue shading to guide you through the service.

The Seder Plate

The leader should review the items on the Seder plate and explain their symbolism, as described on page 5.

Our Seder plate also places matzah in the center, under a cover. We eat matzah on Passover to remind us that our ancestors didn't have time to let their dough rise in their hurry to leave Egypt.

Elijah's Cup — Try this tradition.
Before the Seder begins, some families pour wine from their Kiddush cups into Elijah's Cup. This tradition encourages everyone at the table to make his or her own personal contribution toward our future redemption.

According to the rabbis, why was a Paschal lamb sacrificed on Passover?
a) Steak cost too much.
b) They took a poll in People Magazine.
c) To use the lamb's wool for ritual clothing.
d) Egyptians worshipped the lamb as a god.

4

The Seder Plate

Just as the word Seder means "order," the Seder plate itself has a prescribed order. While the traditional arrangement places the maror near the center of the plate, some of today's Seder plates spread the symbols around the rim of the plate, as shown below and on page four.

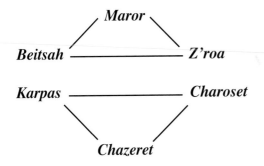

The Seder plate's two triangles.

The top triangle (*beitsah*, *z'roa* and *maror*) consists of symbols ordained in the Torah, while the symbols in the bottom triangle (*karpas*, *charoset*, and *chazeret*) were developed by the rabbis for the Seder ritual.

The typical Seder plate contains five symbols of *Pesach* and our lives as slaves in Egypt:

בֵּיצָה (Beitsah)
The roasted egg reminds us of the roasted sacrifices brought to the Temple in honor of *Pesach*, *Shavuot* and *Sukkot*.

זְרוֹעַ (Z'roa)
The roasted bone reminds us of the Paschal lamb that was brought to the Temple as a sacrifice to God. Until the destruction of the Second Temple in 70 C.E. and the end of religious sacrifices, the Passover meal featured the Paschal lamb. Today, the Passover sacrifice is symbolized on our Seder plate with the *z'roa*. Some vegetarians use a roasted beet instead of the roasted bone.

מָרוֹר (Maror)
The bitter herbs, usually horseradish, remind us of our bitter lives as slaves in Egypt.

כַּרְפַּס (Karpas)
The vegetable, usually green, such as parsley or celery, reminds us that *Pesach* takes place during Spring, a time of rebirth, when crops begin to grow. Some families use radishes or potatoes.

חֲרוֹסֶת (Charoset)
This mixture of apples, nuts, wine and spices reminds us of the mortar used by our ancestors to make bricks for Pharaoh's buildings.

Some Seder plates also have חֲזֶרֶת (Chazeret). Since the Torah tells us to eat bitter *herbs*, a plural word, some prepare a second bitter herb, such as a bitter lettuce (romaine).

What's with the orange on the Seder plate?
Reportedly, a man complained about women's growing involvement in Torah study and synagogue leadership. He declared, "Women have as much place on the bimah as an orange on a Seder plate!" In symbolic protest, the orange has become a popular addition to Seder plates.

Where do you keep your lamb?
The Torah commands us to keep a Paschal lamb at our house for four days before Pesach, then sacrifice it and, later, eat it at the Seder. Since the first Passover took place in Egypt, where people worshipped lambs as gods, the rabbis say it took a lot of courage to carry out this ritual. It's even possible that some Israelites may have hidden the lambs in their houses! Where do you keep yours?

Lighting the Candles

הַדְלָקַת הַנֵּרֹת

Before sunset, light the candles and recite:

Praised are You, Adonai our God, Ruler of the universe, who sanctified us with commandments and commanded us to light the (Shabbat and) festival lights.

בָּרוּךְ אַתָּה יְיָ, אֱלֹהֵינוּ מֶלֶךְ הָעוֹלָם, אֲשֶׁר קִדְּשָׁנוּ בְּמִצְוֹתָיו וְצִוָּנוּ לְהַדְלִיק נֵר שֶׁל (שַׁבָּת וְשֶׁל) יוֹם טוֹב:

Baruch atah Adonai, Eloheinu Melech ha'olam, asher kid'shanu b'mitzvo'tav v'tzivanu l'hadlik ner shel (Shabbat v'shel) yom tov.

She'hecheyanu
Giving Thanks

שֶׁהֶחֱיָנוּ

If you recite the She'hecheyanu here, you do not need to say it again during the Kiddush.

Praised are You, Adonai our God, Ruler of the universe, for giving us life, sustaining us and enabling us to reach this festival season.

בָּרוּךְ אַתָּה יְיָ, אֱלֹהֵינוּ מֶלֶךְ הָעוֹלָם, שֶׁהֶחֱיָנוּ וְקִיְּמָנוּ וְהִגִּיעָנוּ לַזְּמַן הַזֶּה:

Baruch atah Adonai, Eloheinu Melech ha'olam, she'hecheyanu v'kiy'manu v'higi'anu laz'man hazeh.

Why do we light two candles?
The Torah provides two slightly different versions of the Fourth Commandment; that's why we light two candles on Shabbat, one for each meaning.

Here are the two versions:
1) Exodus 20:8 says, "Remember the Sabbath day;" 2) Deuteronomy 5:12 reads, "Observe the Sabbath Day." The practice of lighting two candles is continued on festivals, as is the tradition of covering your eyes during the blessing. (Read the paragraph on the right explaining why we cover our eyes to light the candles; it might surprise you!)

Why do we cover our eyes to light the candles?
When we light the candles, we first perform the mitzvah, then recite the blessing. This is different from most mitzvot, such as the Kiddush, when we first recite the blessing, then drink the wine.

Here's why: Since we would not be allowed to kindle fire on Shabbat, we first light the candles, then cover our eyes and recite the blessing. When we uncover our eyes, we see the candles burning, and it's "as if" we recited the blessing before the performance of the mitzvah. It's "kosher," really!

Kiddush (1st step)
The First Cup of Wine

קַדֵּשׁ

The first cup of wine recalls God's promise, "I will free you from under the burdens of the Egyptians" (Exodus 6:6).

If it's Shabbat, begin the Kiddush with this paragraph in parenthesis, which recalls Creation and God's day of rest on the seventh day. That day of rest later became our Shabbat.

(And there was evening and there was morning — the sixth day. The heavens and the earth, and all their contents, were completed. On the seventh day, God completed the work of creation and rested on the seventh day from all the work God had done. And God blessed the seventh day and made it holy, for on that day God rested from all the work of creation.)

(וַיְהִי עֶרֶב וַיְהִי בֹקֶר, יוֹם הַשִּׁשִּׁי,
וַיְכֻלּוּ הַשָּׁמַיִם וְהָאָרֶץ וְכָל-צְבָאָם:
וַיְכַל אֱלֹהִים בַּיּוֹם הַשְּׁבִיעִי, מְלַאכְתּוֹ אֲשֶׁר עָשָׂה,
וַיִּשְׁבֹּת בַּיּוֹם הַשְּׁבִיעִי, מִכָּל-מְלַאכְתּוֹ אֲשֶׁר עָשָׂה:
וַיְבָרֶךְ אֱלֹהִים אֶת יוֹם הַשְּׁבִיעִי, וַיְקַדֵּשׁ אֹתוֹ, כִּי בוֹ
שָׁבַת מִכָּל-מְלַאכְתּוֹ, אֲשֶׁר-בָּרָא אֱלֹהִים לַעֲשׂוֹת:)

With your permission, my masters and teachers:

סַבְרִי מָרָנָן וְרַבָּנָן וְרַבּוֹתַי:

Praised are You, Adonai our God, Ruler of the universe, who creates the fruit of the vine.

 בָּרוּךְ אַתָּה יְיָ, אֱלֹהֵינוּ מֶלֶךְ הָעוֹלָם, בּוֹרֵא פְּרִי הַגָּפֶן:

Baruch atah Adonai, Eloheinu Melech ha'olam, borei p'ri hagafen.

(Add the words in parenthesis on Shabbat)

Praised are You, Adonai our God, Ruler of the universe, who has chosen us from among all peoples and sanctified us through Your commandments. Lovingly, You have given us (Shabbat for rest and) festivals for rejoicing, seasons and holidays for happiness, including (this Shabbat and) this Festival of Matzot, the season of our liberation, a day of sacred assembly to commemorate the Exodus from Egypt. You have chosen us and sanctified us among all peoples, and You have granted us (the Shabbat and) Your sacred festivals (in love and favor and) in joy and happiness. Praised are You, Adonai, who sanctifies (the Shabbat and) the people Israel and the festival seasons.

בָּרוּךְ אַתָּה יְיָ, אֱלֹהֵינוּ מֶלֶךְ הָעוֹלָם, אֲשֶׁר בָּחַר בָּנוּ
מִכָּל עָם וְרוֹמְמָנוּ מִכָּל לָשׁוֹן, וְקִדְּשָׁנוּ בְּמִצְוֹתָיו.
וַתִּתֶּן-לָנוּ יְיָ אֱלֹהֵינוּ בְּאַהֲבָה (שַׁבָּתוֹת לִמְנוּחָה וּ)
מוֹעֲדִים לְשִׂמְחָה, חַגִּים וּזְמַנִּים לְשָׂשׂוֹן
אֶת-יוֹם (הַשַּׁבָּת הַזֶּה וְאֶת-יוֹם) חַג הַמַּצּוֹת הַזֶּה.
זְמַן חֵרוּתֵנוּ, (בְּאַהֲבָה,) מִקְרָא קֹדֶשׁ,
זֵכֶר לִיצִיאַת מִצְרָיִם. כִּי בָנוּ בָחַרְתָּ וְאוֹתָנוּ קִדַּשְׁתָּ
מִכָּל-הָעַמִּים. (וְשַׁבָּת) וּמוֹעֲדֵי קָדְשֶׁךָ
(בְּאַהֲבָה וּבְרָצוֹן) בְּשִׂמְחָה וּבְשָׂשׂוֹן הִנְחַלְתָּנוּ:
בָּרוּךְ אַתָּה יְיָ, מְקַדֵּשׁ (הַשַּׁבָּת וְ)יִשְׂרָאֵל וְהַזְּמַנִּים:

Don't drink the wine yet!
First, turn to the next page.

Havdalah
The Transition from Shabbat

הַבְדָּלָה

- *If the Seder is on a Saturday night, Havdalah is included with the Kiddush.*

- *If it's not Saturday night, Havdalah is not included; just recite the She'hecheyanu below.*

Using the light from the Yom Tov candles:
recite the blessing,
bend your fingers down into your palms,
then turn your hands toward the candles.

As you hold your hands to the light, note the distinction between light and shadow. Havdalah marks the distinction and transition from Shabbat to an ordinary day of the week.

Praised are You, our God, Ruler of the universe, who creates the lights of fire.

בָּרוּךְ אַתָּה יְיָ, אֱלֹהֵינוּ מֶלֶךְ הָעוֹלָם,
בּוֹרֵא מְאוֹרֵי הָאֵשׁ:

Baruch atah Adonai, Eloheinu Melech ha'olam, borei m'orei ha'eish.

Praised are You, Adonai our God, Ruler of the universe, who distinguishes between the sacred and the secular, between light and darkness, between Israel and the other nations, between the seventh day and the six days of work. You have made a distinction between the holiness of Shabbat and the holiness of the festivals, and sanctified Shabbat more than the six days of work. You have distinguished and sanctified Your people Israel through Your holiness. Praised are You, Adonai, who distinguishes between the holiness of Shabbat and the holiness of *Yom Tov.*

בָּרוּךְ אַתָּה יְיָ, אֱלֹהֵינוּ מֶלֶךְ הָעוֹלָם,
הַמַּבְדִּיל בֵּין קֹדֶשׁ לְחֹל בֵּין אוֹר לְחֹשֶׁךְ,
בֵּין יִשְׂרָאֵל לָעַמִּים, בֵּין יוֹם הַשְּׁבִיעִי לְשֵׁשֶׁת יְמֵי
הַמַּעֲשֶׂה. בֵּין קְדֻשַּׁת שַׁבָּת לִקְדֻשַּׁת יוֹם
טוֹב הִבְדַּלְתָּ וְאֶת-יוֹם הַשְּׁבִיעִי מִשֵּׁשֶׁת
יְמֵי הַמַּעֲשֶׂה קִדַּשְׁתָּ. הִבְדַּלְתָּ וְקִדַּשְׁתָּ
אֶת-עַמְּךָ יִשְׂרָאֵל בִּקְדֻשָּׁתֶךָ.
בָּרוּךְ אַתָּה יְיָ, הַמַּבְדִּיל בֵּין קֹדֶשׁ לְקֹדֶשׁ:

She'hecheyanu
Giving Thanks

שֶׁהֶחֱיָנוּ

Praised are You, Adonai our God, Ruler of the universe, for giving us life, sustaining us and enabling us to reach this festival season.

Now, finally, we can drink the first cup of wine.

בָּרוּךְ אַתָּה יְיָ, אֱלֹהֵינוּ מֶלֶךְ הָעוֹלָם,
שֶׁהֶחֱיָנוּ וְקִיְּמָנוּ וְהִגִּיעָנוּ לַזְּמַן הַזֶּה:

Baruch atah Adonai, Eloheinu Melech ha'olam, she'hecheyanu v'kiy'manu v'higi'anu laz'man hazeh.

8

Fun Facts about the *Kiddush*

Four cups of wine... four promises by God.
We drink wine on Shabbat and all festivals, including Passover, because it is a symbol of joy. Each of the four cups of wine represents a distinct promise of our redemption from slavery in Egypt, as noted in Exodus 6:6-7. As we drink each cup, we should remind ourselves of its special significance, in which God promised:

*1) I will **free** you from the Egyptians' burdens.*
*2) I will **deliver** you from bondage.*
*3) I will **redeem** you with an outstretched arm.*
*4) I will **take** you to be My people.*

Interestingly, some call Elijah's Cup the "Fifth Cup," noting the phrase in Exodus 6:8, "And I will bring you into the land."

The Exodus — it's always in there!
In every Kiddush, we remember the "y'tziat Mitzrayim" (יְצִיאַת מִצְרַיִם), which means the "Exodus from Egypt." That phrase is in every Kiddush, whether it's Shabbat, Pesach, or any other Jewish festival.

On Shabbat, we add some Torah to the Kiddush.
The Shabbat Kiddush (including the Kiddush for Pesach and other festivals) begins with verses from Genesis 1:31 and 2:1-3. In these verses, God rested on the seventh day after creating the world and made it a holy day. Today, the seventh day is our Shabbat. You can even read this part with Torah trope!

Fun Facts about *Havdalah*

What is the significance of Havdalah?
Havdalah is said at the end of Shabbat to mark the distinction and transition from Shabbat to an ordinary day of the week. We recite the blessings over wine, spices and fire to prepare for the dramatic change from the peacefulness of Shabbat to the hectic pace of ordinary life. Of course, at the Passover Seder, Havdalah marks the distinction and transition from Shabbat to a holy day.

Why is this Havdalah different?
On a typical Havdalah, we recite blessings over wine, spices and fire. But during the Passover Havdalah, we only recite the blessing over fire. Moreover, we use the Yom Tov candles for fire, not a special Havdalah candle. The blessing over wine is not recited, since Havdalah is already included in the Kiddush. Also, we do not recite the blessing over spices, since it would only be said when Shabbat is followed by an ordinary day. The Passover Havdalah marks the transition from Shabbat to Yom Tov.

When Shabbat is followed by an ordinary day (not a festival, like Passover), why do we recite a blessing over spices and sniff them during *Havdalah*?
a) According to tradition, Jewish boxers sniffed spices after getting knocked out.
b) After Shabbat, we lose our extra soul.
c) To use them later in our evening dinner.
d) To prepare for a fun Saturday night.

When it's Shabbat (but not Pesach), why do we use a Havdalah candle with two wicks?
The Havdalah prayer thanks God for creating the "lights of fire." Since "lights" is plural, two candles were used originally in the Havdalah ceremony. Today, we usually use one braided candle with two or more wicks, rather than the two candles. Of course, at the Passover Seder, we use our Yom Tov candles as the lights of fire, instead of a Havdalah candle.

Urchatz (2nd step)
Wash Your Hands

וּרְחַץ

Wash your hands without reciting a blessing.

Karpas (3rd step)
Dip a Vegetable

כַּרְפַּס

Dip a vegetable in salt water and recite:

Praised are You, Adonai our God, Ruler of the universe, who creates the fruit of the earth.

Now, we eat the vegetable.

 בָּרוּךְ אַתָּה יְיָ, אֱלֹהֵינוּ מֶלֶךְ הָעוֹלָם,
בּוֹרֵא פְּרִי הָאֲדָמָה:

Baruch atah Adonai, Eloheinu Melech ha'olam, borei p'ri ha'adamah.

Any Questions Yet?

Passover is filled with unusual customs; we just did two of them.
Why are we doing these things?
Ask questions, it's a sign of our freedom!

Why do we wash our hands twice during the Seder; once with a blessing, once without?
The hand washing for Urchatz is more of an old world custom than a religious ritual — that's why there's no blessing. Long ago, it was common to wash your hands at the table before dipping food into a liquid or sauce, such as dipping karpas into salt water. Later, in the Seder's sixth step, Rochtzah, we will recite a blessing as we wash our hands, much as the priests washed their hands before approaching the altar in the Temple.

Will the real karpas please stand up?
Today, we use most any kind of vegetable to symbolize karpas, although it is usually green. But really, what is karpas? It's an Aramaic form of a Greek word, which the Talmud defines as petrozel. Today, it's commonly thought to be parsley. Some believe the karpas also recalls the hyssop plant, which was used to spread lamb's blood on our ancestors' doorposts so the tenth plague would pass over their houses.

Yachatz (4th step)
Break the Middle Matzah

יַחַץ

Yachatz means "break in half," so let's break away! From the plate with the three matzot:

1) Take the middle matzah and break it in two.

2) Place the larger piece in a napkin or bag, and set it aside as the *Afikoman*. This will be eaten at the end of the meal.

3) Place the smaller piece between the other two matzot.

4) Now, hide the *Afikoman*! Later, in the 11th step, *Tzafun*, we will find the *Afikoman* and eat it. The *Afikoman* is the last thing we eat all night. *Tzafun* actually means "hidden."

There's more to matzah than just great taste.
Matzah is one of Passover's most important symbols. In fact, the Torah contains several verses in which we are commanded to eat matzah on Passover.

Matzah is the "bread of affliction," a symbol of our ancestors' poverty and slavery in Egypt. In a deeper sense, the rabbis view matzah as a humble bread, a symbol of purity. By contrast, leavened bread (chametz) rises and becomes "puffed up," and is said to represent man's arrogance. While we should enjoy our freedom, we should never become puffed up and always be careful to maintain our humility.

Why do we break the middle matzah?
a) It's going to break anyway.
b) To honor ancient Jewish karate experts.
c) To create the *Afikoman*.
d) To save the other half for later.

Why do we use three matzot?
On Shabbat and most festivals, we use two loaves to remind us of the double portion of manna the Israelites received every sixth day of the week as they wandered through the desert. With a double portion, they didn't have to gather manna on Shabbat, the day of rest.

The two matzot signifying the double portion of manna will be used later for the Motzi Matzah. The third matzah is used for the Yachatz, in which we break the matzah for the Afikoman. Some suggest the three matzot represent the three ancient divisions of Jewish people: Priests (Kohanim), Levites and Israelites.

Why do we place the *Afikoman* in a napkin or a bag before it is hidden?
a) It's an old trick created by James Bond.
b) Pharaoh tried to steal the *Afikoman*.
c) The Israelites wrapped up their dough.
d) Who would think to look in a napkin or bag?

11

Ha Lachma Anya
The Bread of Affliction

הָא לַחְמָא עַנְיָא

The difficult experiences of our ancestors in Egypt should make us sensitive to the needs of others on *Pesach*. *Ha Lachma Anya* tells us that all Jewish people, regardless of whether they are hungry or in need, should have the opportunity to celebrate Passover. As such, it is a *mitzvah* to invite those who are hungry or in need to join you at your table.

Uncover the matzot.

This is the bread of affliction, which our ancestors ate in the land of Egypt. Let all who are hungry, come and eat. Let all who are in need, come and celebrate Passover. This year, we are here. Next year, may we be in the land of Israel. This year, we are slaves. Next year, may we be free.

הָא לַחְמָא עַנְיָא,
דִּי אֲכָלוּ אַבְהָתָנָא בְּאַרְעָא דְמִצְרָיִם.
כָּל דִּכְפִין יֵיתֵי וְיֵכוֹל, כָּל דִּצְרִיךְ יֵיתֵי וְיִפְסַח.
הָשַׁתָּא הָכָא, לְשָׁנָה הַבָּאָה בְּאַרְעָא דְיִשְׂרָאֵל.
הָשַׁתָּא עַבְדֵי, לְשָׁנָה הַבָּאָה בְּנֵי חוֹרִין:

Ha lachma anya, di achalu av'hatana b'ar'a d'mitzrayim. Kol dich'fin yeitei v'yeichol, kol ditz'rich yeitei v'yifsach. Hashata hacha, l'shanah haba'ah b'ar'a d'yisrael. Hashata avdei, l'shanah haba'ah b'nei chorin.

Hebrew isn't the Haggadah's only language!
Ha Lachma Anya is written in Aramaic, which was spoken by our ancestors in the 2nd century B.C.E., when many parts of the Haggadah were written. Since Ha Lachma Anya invites everyone who is hungry to celebrate Passover in our homes, it's in Aramaic so everyone would understand.

The tradition of Maot Chittim.
Maot Chittim means "money for wheat." In this tradition, we gather matzah, wine and a variety of other Passover foods and items, and distribute them to the needy so all Jews can celebrate the festival. This is in keeping with an important theme of Passover, "Let all who are hungry, come and eat."

Why are there tiny holes in matzah?
a) Matzah is holy food.
b) To keep the matzah dough from rising.
c) To bring out matzah's wonderful taste.
d) Tradition!

What does *chametz* actually mean?
a) Junk
b) Sour
c) Bread
d) Spoiled bread, oozing with mold.

The Four Questions

מַה נִּשְׁתַּנָּה

Cover the matzot.

Why is this night different from all other nights?

מַה נִּשְׁתַּנָּה הַלַּיְלָה הַזֶּה מִכָּל הַלֵּילוֹת?

Ma nishtanah halailah hazeh, mikol haleilot?

1) On all other nights,
   we eat either bread or matzah.
   On this night, why do we eat only matzah?

שֶׁבְּכָל הַלֵּילוֹת אָנוּ אוֹכְלִין חָמֵץ וּמַצָּה.
הַלַּיְלָה הַזֶּה כֻּלּוֹ מַצָּה:

Sheb'chol haleilot, anu ochlin, chameitz u'matzah.
Halailah hazeh, kulo matzah.

2) On all other nights,
   we eat any kind of vegetable.
   On this night, why do we eat bitter herbs?

שֶׁבְּכָל הַלֵּילוֹת אָנוּ אוֹכְלִין שְׁאָר יְרָקוֹת.
הַלַּיְלָה הַזֶּה מָרוֹר:

Sheb'chol haleilot, anu ochlin, sh'ar y'rakot.
Halailah hazeh, maror.

3) On all other nights,
   we usually don't dip our foods even once.
   On this night, why do we dip our foods twice?

שֶׁבְּכָל הַלֵּילוֹת אֵין אָנוּ מַטְבִּילִין
אֲפִילוּ פַּעַם אֶחָת. הַלַּיְלָה הַזֶּה שְׁתֵּי פְעָמִים:

Sheb'chol haleilot, ein anu mat'bilin,
a'filu pa'am echat. Halailah hazeh, sh'tei f'amim.

4) On all other nights,
   we eat either sitting upright or reclining.
   On this night, why do we recline as we eat?

שֶׁבְּכָל הַלֵּילוֹת אָנוּ אוֹכְלִין בֵּין יוֹשְׁבִין
וּבֵין מְסֻבִּין. הַלַּיְלָה הַזֶּה כֻּלָּנוּ מְסֻבִּין:

Sheb'chol haleilot, anu ochlin, bein yoshvin u'vein
m'subin. Halailah hazeh, kulanu m'subin.

Times have changed... so have the Questions!
The original third question asked why we only eat roasted meat, which referred to the sacrificed Paschal lamb. But when the Second Temple was destroyed in 70 C.E., Jews stopped the practice of religious sacrifices. As a result, the roasted meat question was eliminated, dipping was moved up to the third question, and reclining was added as the fourth question.

Where are the answers?
The Four Questions are not answered directly in the Haggadah because we are supposed to find the answers for ourselves. This is another way in which the Haggadah encourages us to search for meaning in the Seder. Make your Seder different. Don't just ask the questions — discuss possible answers among yourselves!

Fun Facts About The Four Questions

What does each Question have in common?
The rituals awaken our senses. The rabbis felt words were not enough to make us fully appreciate Passover — we need to re-live our ancestors' experience through our senses — hearing, tasting and smelling. The Questions also involve unusual customs, which encourage more questions and more learning.

Translated directly from Hebrew, how many "Questions" are actually in the traditional Haggadah text?
a) You're kidding, right? Four!
b) Three
c) Two
d) One

There's a "left" way to recline.
Most everyone knows that you should recline during the Passover meal. But you shouldn't just recline — you should lean to the left. Among the many reasons offered, here's a practical one: if you're right-handed, leaning to the left frees your right hand for eating.   As slaves, we couldn't lean or recline.

Why is four a common number in Passover?
We have four questions, four children, and four cups of wine. While the four cups of wine relate to God's four promises in Exodus 6:6-7, some believe the Haggadah's use of the number four may be in honor of the four Matriarchs: Sarah, Rebecca, Rachel and Leah. Beginning with Sarah, women have led the observance of Jewish traditions in the home, even against great odds — even during the slavery in Egypt.

The Four Children

The Haggadah writers created this section to appeal to various types of children in ways they can understand.

What does the wise child ask?
"Could you explain the meaning of Passover?"
This child is truly interested in understanding the meaning of Passover. You should explain the laws of Passover in great detail, including the law that one may not eat anything after the *Afikoman.*

What does the wicked child ask?
"What is the purpose of Passover? Since it has no meaning to me, why bother with the Seder?"
This child excludes himself from the Jewish community and the basic principles of Judaism. You should speak sharply to the child, "This is done because of what God did for me when I went out from Egypt. For *me*, but not for *him* (the wicked child); had he (the wicked child) been there, he would not have been freed."

What does the simple child ask?
"What is Passover all about?"
This child wants to learn about Passover, but needs help in understanding. Every child deserves the opportunity to learn about Passover and appreciate its meaning. You should tell the child, "We celebrate Passover because God brought us out of Egypt and freed us from slavery."

As for the child who does not know how to ask:
This child may want to understand Passover, but might need help in getting started. Therefore, you need to begin the discussion by telling the child, "We celebrate Passover because of what God did for me when I went out from Egypt."

Including the girls... it's about time!
Early Haggadot called this section, "The Four Sons." In recent years, some Haggadot have changed the name to "The Four Children." This is an important change, especially given women's increasing involvement in Torah study as well as synagogue ritual and leadership.

Four responses, but one main message.
The Four Children section might express the reason for celebrating Passover in four different ways, but the message is essentially the same: to appreciate "what God did for me when I went out from Egypt." This message from Exodus 13:8 applies to all children, although the approach is customized in this section to meet their individual needs.

Are you a "wicked" child? Take the test!
The commentators don't view the wicked child as a mean person; they look at the factors listed below. Check how you rate with the answers on page 46. With respect to Passover, do you:
a) Think the Seder is a burden?
b) Feel the rituals are outdated and irrelevant?
c) Question the need for the religious service?
d) Believe the miracles were coincidences?

Maggid (5th step)
Tell the Passover Story

(Children's Version)

*(Note: a more complete version of the
Passover Story begins on page 19.)*

Uncover the matzot.

Today, most Jewish people are free to live their
lives as they wish. But more than three thousand
years ago, our people, the Israelites, were slaves
in Egypt.

For hundreds of years, they were forced to work
long, hard days in the hot desert sun. Against
their will, they made bricks and built cities for
Pharaoh, the king of Egypt. It was a terrible
time for our people. *(Song #1)*

There seemed to be no hope. Only a miracle
could save the Israelites. They got more than a
miracle; they got help from God. Here's how it
happened:

One day, a shepherd named Moses was tending
to his sheep. He saw a bush burning in the
wilderness. Instead of turning to ashes, the bush
kept burning. Curious, Moses went toward the
bush. There, he heard the voice of God. Moses
was told to deliver a very important message to
Pharaoh: Let my people go! *(Song #2)*

(Song #1)
Bang, Bang, Bang
Bang, bang, bang,
Hold your hammer low.
Bang, bang, bang,
Give a heavy blow.
For it's work, work, work,
Every day and every night.
For it's work, work, work,
When it's dark and when it's light.

Imagine: What if you were a slave?
*What if you worked all day and didn't have time
to play? What if you couldn't eat fun foods like
cookies and pizza, but had to eat matzah all the
time? And it wasn't just for a day or a week, but
every single day of your life! How would you
feel? What a rotten life! Then, how would you
feel to finally be free?*

(Song #2)
Let My People Go
When Israel was in Egypt land.
Let my people go.
Oppressed so hard they could not stand.
Let my people go.
Go down, Moses, way down to Egypt land.
Tell old Pharaoh, "Let my people go!"

מַגִּיד

Moses and his brother, Aaron, went to Pharaoh. They told Pharaoh that God wanted our people to be freed from slavery. But Pharaoh wouldn't listen. He didn't believe in God. Pharaoh believed in idols, which were statues made of stone. He wouldn't free our people. *(Song #3)*

To make Pharaoh free the slaves, God sent ten plagues, one after the other. In the first plague, the Nile River turned to blood. The Egyptians couldn't drink water or wash. Then a second plague struck: frogs! *(Song #4)*.

One plague after the next punished the Egyptian people, but Pharaoh would not free the slaves. Finally, after ten plagues, Pharaoh gave up and freed the slaves!

In their hurry to leave Egypt, the Israelites didn't have time to let their bread rise. So they ate a flat bread called *matzah*. As they traveled through the desert, they lived in huts, called *sukkot*. When they ran out of food, God sent manna raining down from the sky to feed them.

After a few days of freedom, the Israelites arrived at the Sea of Reeds. Suddenly, they saw the Egyptian army speeding toward them. The Israelites were trapped against the sea, with nowhere to go! They needed another miracle, and they got one. God parted the sea into two walls of water, and the Israelites walked across safely on dry land! Now, finally, they were free!

Today, on Passover, we thank God for our freedom. Without God's help, we might still be slaves.

(Song #3)
Listen, King Pharaoh
Oh listen, oh listen, oh listen, King Pharaoh.
Oh listen, oh listen, please let my people go.
They want to go away,
they work too hard each day,
King Pharaoh, King Pharaoh,
What do you say?
No, no, no, I will not let them go!
No, no, no, I will not let them go!

(Song #4)
The Frog Song
One morning when Pharaoh awoke in his bed,
There were frogs on his head
and frogs in his bed,
Frogs on his nose and frogs on his toes,
Frogs here, frogs there,
Frogs were jumping everywhere!

Songs #1, #3 and #4 are from *Passover Music Box,* words and music by Shirley R. Cohen © 1951 Kinor Records. Song #2 is an old spiritual song.

Can toys become idols?
All of us love toys. But have you ever loved a toy too much? Did you make it more important than your family or friends? When that happens, we turn our toys into idols, and that's against the spirit of Passover. Toys are a lot of fun, but we should remember that they are just things, and people are always more important.

"And Moses said to the people, 'Fear not, stand still, and witness the deliverance, which Adonai will work for you today...' "
Exodus 14:13

"And the children of Israel went into the midst of the sea upon the dry ground; and the waters were a wall on their right hand and on their left."
Exodus 14:22

Tell the Passover Story
The Traditional Beginnings

מַגִּיד

Avadim Hayinu: *We Were Slaves*

עֲבָדִים הָיִינוּ

We were slaves to Pharaoh in Egypt, but Adonai our God brought us out from there with a mighty hand and an outstretched arm. If the Holy One, who is to be praised, had not brought our ancestors out from Egypt, then we, our children, and our children's children, would still be enslaved to Pharaoh in Egypt. Therefore, even if all of us were wise, even if all of us possessed great understanding and experience, even if all of us were learned in the Torah, it would still be our duty to tell the story of the Exodus from Egypt. The more one elaborates upon the story of the Exodus, the more praise is deserved.

עֲבָדִים הָיִינוּ לְפַרְעֹה בְּמִצְרָיִם.
וַיּוֹצִיאֵנוּ יְיָ אֱלֹהֵינוּ מִשָּׁם, בְּיָד חֲזָקָה
וּבִזְרוֹעַ נְטוּיָה, וְאִלּוּ לֹא הוֹצִיא
הַקָּדוֹשׁ בָּרוּךְ הוּא אֶת־אֲבוֹתֵינוּ מִמִּצְרַיִם,
הֲרֵי אָנוּ וּבָנֵינוּ וּבְנֵי בָנֵינוּ,
מְשֻׁעְבָּדִים הָיִינוּ לְפַרְעֹה בְּמִצְרָיִם.
וַאֲפִילוּ כֻּלָּנוּ חֲכָמִים, כֻּלָּנוּ נְבוֹנִים,
כֻּלָּנוּ זְקֵנִים, כֻּלָּנוּ יוֹדְעִים אֶת־הַתּוֹרָה,
מִצְוָה עָלֵינוּ לְסַפֵּר בִּיצִיאַת מִצְרָיִם. וְכָל
הַמַּרְבֶּה לְסַפֵּר בִּיצִיאַת מִצְרַיִם, הֲרֵי זֶה מְשֻׁבָּח:

Mit'chilah: *In the Beginning*

מִתְּחִלָה

In the beginning, our ancestors worshipped idols. But later, we were brought to God's service. As it is written, "And Joshua said to all the people, 'Thus says Adonai, God of Israel: Long ago your ancestors, including Terach, the father of Abraham and Nachor, lived beyond the Euphrates River. They served other gods. Then I took your father Abraham from beyond the River, and led him through all the land of Canaan. I multiplied his descendants and gave him Isaac. To Isaac, I gave Jacob and Esau; and to Esau, I gave Mount Seir as his inheritance. And, Jacob and his children went down to Egypt" (Joshua 24:2-4).

מִתְּחִלָה עוֹבְדֵי עֲבוֹדָה זָרָה הָיוּ אֲבוֹתֵינוּ.
וְעַכְשָׁו קֵרְבָנוּ הַמָּקוֹם לַעֲבוֹדָתוֹ. שֶׁנֶּאֱמַר: וַיֹּאמֶר
יְהוֹשֻׁעַ אֶל־כָּל־הָעָם. כֹּה אָמַר יְיָ אֱלֹהֵי יִשְׂרָאֵל:
בְּעֵבֶר הַנָּהָר יָשְׁבוּ אֲבוֹתֵיכֶם מֵעוֹלָם, תֶּרַח אֲבִי
אַבְרָהָם וַאֲבִי נָחוֹר. וַיַּעַבְדוּ אֱלֹהִים אֲחֵרִים:
וָאֶקַּח אֶת־אֲבִיכֶם אֶת־אַבְרָהָם מֵעֵבֶר הַנָּהָר,
וָאוֹלֵךְ אוֹתוֹ בְּכָל־אֶרֶץ כְּנָעַן. וָאַרְבֶּה אֶת־זַרְעוֹ,
וָאֶתֶּן לוֹ אֶת־יִצְחָק: וָאֶתֵּן לְיִצְחָק אֶת־יַעֲקֹב
וְאֶת־עֵשָׂו. וָאֶתֵּן לְעֵשָׂו אֶת־הַר שֵׂעִיר,
לָרֶשֶׁת אוֹתוֹ. וְיַעֲקֹב וּבָנָיו יָרְדוּ מִצְרָיִם:

Praised be God who keeps the promise made to Israel. Praised be God, who planned our enslavement and liberation as promised in the covenant with our father Abraham. As it is written, "God said to Abram, 'Know for certain that your descendants will be strangers in a strange land, and will be enslaved and treated harshly for four hundred years. But I will judge the nation they served and afterward they will leave with great wealth' " (Genesis 15:13-14).

בָּרוּךְ שׁוֹמֵר הַבְטָחָתוֹ לְיִשְׂרָאֵל. בָּרוּךְ הוּא. שֶׁהַקָּדוֹשׁ
בָּרוּךְ הוּא חִשַּׁב אֶת־הַקֵּץ, לַעֲשׂוֹת כְּמָה שֶׁאָמַר
לְאַבְרָהָם אָבִינוּ בִּבְרִית בֵּין הַבְּתָרִים, שֶׁנֶּאֱמַר:
וַיֹּאמֶר לְאַבְרָם יָדֹעַ תֵּדַע, כִּי־גֵר יִהְיֶה זַרְעֶךָ,
בְּאֶרֶץ לֹא לָהֶם, וַעֲבָדוּם וְעִנּוּ אֹתָם
אַרְבַּע מֵאוֹת שָׁנָה: וְגַם אֶת־הַגּוֹי אֲשֶׁר
יַעֲבֹדוּ דָּן אָנֹכִי, וְאַחֲרֵי כֵן יֵצְאוּ, בִּרְכֻשׁ גָּדוֹל:

Maggid (5th step)
Tell the Passover Story

מַגִּיד

The Passover Story from the Torah

Uncover the matzot. Note: Moses is included in this Haggadah to provide a more complete story. See the explanation at the bottom of this column.

On Passover, we remember how God freed our ancestors from slavery more than 3,000 years ago. God reached out with "a mighty hand and an outstretched arm" and led the Israelites to freedom. Without God's help, we might still be slaves.

Long before the time of Passover, Abraham began the Jewish worship of one God, instead of idols. In return, God made a covenant with Abraham that his descendants would be great and numerous, but they would become slaves in a foreign land for four hundred years and then be freed.

Generations later, a famine struck Canaan, the homeland of Jacob, Abraham's grandson. Jacob led his extended family, the children of Israel, into Egypt to find a better supply of food. Beginning with the great accomplishments of Jacob's son, Joseph, the Israelites assumed an increasingly important role in Egyptian society. However, years later, a new Pharaoh came to power in Egypt. He feared the success and growing size of the Israelite population, and placed them into slavery.

The Passover story is found in *Sh'mot*, the second book of the Torah. This book is called Exodus in English, a Greek word meaning "The Departure." What does *Sh'mot* mean?
a) Names
b) Addresses
c) Phone Numbers
d) The Departure

Why does the name Moses only appear once in the traditional Haggadah?
While Moses led our ancestors out of Egypt, he was merely a messenger for God, who truly freed the slaves with the Ten Plagues and the parting of the sea. Given our past experience with the golden calf, the original Haggadah writers feared we would turn Moses into an idol and worship him. That's why the name Moses only appears once in the traditional Haggadah!

Do miracles still happen?
The Passover story speaks about miracles, such as the parting of the sea. But are miracles all in the past? Do they still happen today? Look around. We've all seen amazing things happen in our lives that are difficult to explain. While it's easy to dismiss these as luck or chance, maybe we shouldn't. Maybe miracles do still happen and we don't always recognize the wonder of God's work.

Our ancestors were slaves for many generations, making bricks and building cities for Pharaoh. As much as Pharaoh tried to destroy the Israelites through hard labor and slavery, their population grew. This led Pharaoh to decree that every Israelite baby boy must be drowned in the Nile River. But the Israelite midwives wouldn't follow the law and secretly hid the baby boys. One of the babies hidden was Moses.

After hiding Moses for the first three months of his life, his mother placed him in a basket among the reeds of the Nile River. The basket was found by Pharaoh's daughter, who named the baby Moses, because she "drew him out of the water." Moses' sister, Miriam, watched Pharaoh's daughter find the baby and arranged to have him nursed by an Israelite midwife, who turned out to be Moses' real mother!

Although Moses was adopted by Pharaoh's daughter and raised in the Egyptian palace, the time spent with his mother and family must have made quite an impression on him. He felt great compassion for the slaves and realized that he too was an Israelite. Unfortunately, in an attempt to stop a slave from being beaten, he killed an Egyptian and had to leave the country.

But Moses would return to Egypt. One day, while working as a shepherd in Midian, Moses saw a bush burning in the wilderness. Strangely, the bush kept burning; it was not consumed. Moses went toward the bush and found himself in the presence of God, who told him to help free the Israelites.

Be proud of who you are.
Although the Israelites lived with the Egyptians for hundreds of years, tradition tells us they maintained their language, religious customs and other qualities that made them unique. While we live in a non-Jewish world, we should be proud of our Jewish heritage and maintain our unique traditions and identity.

Courageous women made freedom possible.
Women played a critical role in gaining the freedom of our ancestors:
- *Moses' sister and mother, Miriam and Yocheved, joined with other midwives to break Pharaoh's law and hide baby boys to save them from drowning;*
- *Pharaoh's daughter rescued Moses from the river, then raised him at the palace, even though she knew he was the son of an Israelite slave.*

Without the courage of these women, Moses might not have had the opportunity to grow up and become the leader of the Israelites.

Mitzrayim **is the Hebrew word for Egypt. What is the real meaning of** *Mitzrayim*?
a) Egypt
b) A narrow place
c) Pharaoh's home
d) Rays of *mitzvot*

Today, the burning bush is a symbol of:
a) Peace
b) Love
c) Israel
d) Y2K

When first told by God to help free the Israelites, Moses replied:
a) "Who me? Why would they listen to me?"
b) "What will I say when they ask Your name?"
c) "Yes, I will lead them to freedom."
d) Moses didn't say anything; he simply bowed.

Note: Answers can now be found on page 47.

Family life is critical to Judaism's survival.
One of Pharaoh's top priorities was to disrupt Jewish family life. When Pharaoh began drowning Jewish baby boys, many fathers divorced their wives, rather than have children who would be killed. One of the men who led this trend was Amram, who after the urging of his daughter, Miriam, remarried his wife, Yocheved. They later had a son named Moses.

Moses and his brother, Aaron, told Pharaoh to free their people, but Pharaoh wouldn't listen.
The Egyptians only worshipped idols and Pharaoh; they couldn't understand the existence of a God they couldn't see. Even Pharaoh thought he was a god who should be worshipped by the Egyptians.

Pharaoh's worship of idols and the slavery of the Israelites led to a series of ten plagues.
After some of the plagues, Pharaoh agreed to free the slaves, then changed his mind and kept them in slavery. So more plagues struck. From the Nile River turning to blood, to an intense darkness that made it impossible to see, the first nine plagues terrified the Egyptian people. But still, Pharaoh wouldn't free the slaves.

It took the tenth plague, the death of the first born, to convince Pharaoh that his gods were merely statues. Pharaoh lost his first-born son in the tenth plague, causing him to realize that neither he nor his statues were gods — there was only one true God. Finally, he freed the slaves.

God's power helped Aaron turn a rod into a snake. How did Pharaoh's magicians do it?
a) No big deal; it's an old Egyptian trick.
b) They learned the trick in Las Vegas.
c) Ancient Egyptian hypnosis.
d) Special snakes.

When Pharaoh's magicians couldn't reproduce the third plague, lice, what did they think?
a) Oh boy, are we in trouble!
b) The plagues must be the finger of God.
c) Quick, someone invent the fly swatter!
d) You scratch my back and I'll scratch yours.

After the tenth plague, Pharaoh realized he wasn't a god to be worshipped, and:
a) Bought a lottery ticket.
b) Looked in the newspaper for a new job.
c) Bowed down and kissed Moses' feet... yuk!
d) Asked Moses and Aaron to bless him.

The Ten Plagues discredited Egypt's system of idolatry.
Some believe that each of the Ten Plagues was aimed at destroying an object of Egyptian idolatry. For example, the first plague, blood, was directed toward the Nile River, which was worshipped by the Egyptians. Similarly, Pharaoh realized that he himself was not a god when the tenth plague killed his son. One by one, the Ten Plagues effectively discredited Egypt's system of idolatry.

The Ten Plagues also affected the Israelites.
The object of the Ten Plagues was not just to punish the Egyptians, it was also to strengthen the Israelites' belief in God. In Exodus 10:2, God tells Moses the plagues are so "that you may know that I am Adonai." The plagues provided very clear evidence to the Israelites that God truly existed. After ten plagues, even Pharaoh believed in God!

Shabbat offers an important balance against modern idolatry.
While it's great to have goals in life and pursue them with hard work and enthusiasm, they shouldn't take over your entire life and, in effect, become an idol of worship. That's one of the great joys of Shabbat — to take a break from our daily pursuits, rest and appreciate life. Try it!

We're still thankful for our first born.
We still remember that God spared our first born in Egypt during the tenth plague through the Pidyon Habben ceremony ("Redeeming the son") on the 31st day of a first-born son's life. Also, the day of Erev Pesach is a fast for the first born. In Exodus 13:2, God tells Moses, "Sanctify unto Me all the first born... it (the first born) is Mine."

The Israelites left Egypt, just as God had promised in the covenant with Abraham. God promised the Egyptians would be judged (with the Ten Plagues) and that Abraham's descendants would leave a foreign land (Egypt) with great wealth. By the time of the Exodus, the 70 Israelites who entered Egypt 400 years earlier had multiplied to 600,000.

In their hurry to leave Egypt, the Israelites didn't have time to let their bread rise. So they ate *matzah*, a flat bread. The Israelites were guided in the desert by God through a cloud by day and a pillar of fire by night.

Within a few days, they arrived at the Sea of Reeds (formerly believed to be the Red Sea). Suddenly, the Egyptian army was in hot pursuit; they wanted the Israelites to return as slaves.

The Israelites were trapped, backed up against the sea. They needed a miracle and they got one. God parted the waters of the sea, with walls of water forming on either side, so the Israelites could pass safely on dry land.

Meanwhile, a pillar of cloud hindered the Egyptian army's entry to the sea. As the Israelites reached dry land, the cloud lifted and the Egyptians quickly rushed in. But when Moses raised his staff, God caused the walls of the sea to collapse. The Egyptian army drowned and didn't threaten Israel for hundreds of years.

Note: The traditional Passover story ends with the crossing at the Sea of Reeds. The rest of this story does not relate directly to Passover; it follows the Israelites into the Promised Land.

Why is the Exodus so important to us?
The Exodus may be the most pivotal event in Judaism. That's when God's presence was revealed to the Israelites and the Jews became the chosen people. Soon after, our ancestors received the Ten Commandments from God. Through this series of events, it has been said that the Jews were transformed from servants of Pharaoh to servants of God.

The Exodus is so important to Judaism, it is mentioned in every:
a) *Kiddush.*
b) Scroll inside a *mezuzah.*
c) Scroll inside *tefilin.*
d) Scroll inside kosher fortune cookies.

Are these just coincidences?
1) Moses: From Reeds to the Sea of Reeds
Moses, who was rescued from the reeds of the Nile River, grew up to lead God's rescue of the Israelites through the Sea of Reeds!

2) The Name Moses Predicted Our Future
Pharaoh's daughter chose the name Moses because she "drew him out of the water." Later, when Moses raised his staff, God parted the sea so the Israelites could cross safely on dry land!

3) Pharaoh's Dream Came True
According to tradition, Pharaoh dreamed that an Israelite boy would grow up and overthrow him — Moses was that boy!

Many scholars now believe the Israelites crossed at the Sea of Reeds, not the Red Sea, because the Torah calls the sea *yam suf*, and *suf* refers to:
a) Surfing, which is wild at the Sea of Reeds.
b) Surfing the Internet, which actually began at the Sea of Reeds.
c) Reeds, which can't grow in the Red Sea.
d) This is crazy! Of course it's the Red Sea!

The two sides of matzah.
Matzah is known as the bread of affliction, since our ancestors ate it during their slavery in Egypt and afterward in their hurry to leave during the Exodus. Unlike bread, matzah is flat, a humble food fit for slaves. But since matzah was also eaten after our ancestors were freed from slavery, isn't matzah also the bread of freedom?

After gaining their freedom, the Israelites arrived at Mount Sinai, where Moses received the Ten Commandments. Moses was up on Mount Sinai for forty days, and some Israelites began to lose their faith in God. When Moses came down from Mount Sinai carrying the Ten Commandments, he saw the Israelites worshipping a golden calf and doing other terrible things. Enraged by the idol worshipping, Moses threw the two stone tablets down the mountainside and broke them. Then he destroyed the golden calf.

Moses soon returned to Mount Sinai and received the Ten Commandments for a second time. To finally rid them of their idolatrous ways and slave mentality, the Israelites wandered the desert for forty years, living in temporary booths called *sukkot*. When food became scarce, God sent manna raining down from the sky to feed the Israelites. God provided a double portion on the sixth day so the Israelites wouldn't have to gather manna on the seventh day, Shabbat, the day of rest.

After forty years of wandering, the Israelites were ready to enter the Promised Land and live according to God's laws, the Ten Commandments and the Torah. Moses handed the Torah to Joshua, who led the Israelites into the Promised Land.

Finally, in 1948, after more than 3,000 years, our Promised Land became the Jewish State, Israel. Today, on Passover, we thank God for leading us to freedom and our Jewish way of life.

Today, the double portion of manna on the sixth day is symbolized by two:
a) Of the three matzot on *Pesach*.
b) Loaves of *challah* on Shabbat.
c) Lulav branches on *Sukkot*.
d) Pizzas on *Purim* (kosher, of course!).

Why didn't Moses enter the Promised Land?
a) He didn't feel he was worthy.
b) He disobeyed God.
c) He struck a rock.
d) He struck oil and moved to Beverly Hills.

Discussion Questions:
Passover is a time to ask questions and engage in lively discussion. Try these questions, if you like. Of course, the best questions will come from the discussion at your own Seder table.

- *Why did the Israelites have to endure so much to receive the Ten Commandments and the Torah? Did this long and difficult period help the Israelites or hurt them?*

- *Why was God so involved with our ancestors during this time? Is God still involved today? Should we want God to intervene in our lives, or should we want to preserve our free choice? Can we have both?*

Want good leadership training?
Be a shepherd!
Before Moses became God's messenger, he worked as a shepherd for Jethro in Midian. Keeping sheep together proved to be good training for his future job as leader of the Israelites. Moses kept the Israelites together for forty years in the desert through revolts, hunger, thirst and other problems so they could finally enter the Promised Land. Interestingly, both Abraham and Jacob were shepherds, too!

Appreciate your freedom.
The freedom we enjoy today has been the work of God and many great people through the ages. We are very fortunate today that most of us are free to observe our Jewish religion and traditions. However, even today, not all of us are free, and the struggle to practice Judaism continues in most every part of the world.

V'hi She'amdah
The Promise

וְהִיא שֶׁעָמְדָה

Long before the Exodus from Egypt, our ancestors worshipped idols. The idol worshipping continued for many generations until Abraham began the worship of one God. In recognition of Abraham's faithfulness, God made a covenant with him and promised:

"Know for certain that your descendants will be strangers in a strange land, and will be enslaved and treated harshly for four hundred years. But I will judge the nation they served and afterward they will leave with great wealth" (Genesis 15:13-14).

God kept that promise. Abraham's descendants were strangers in a strange land — Egypt. Our people lived in Egypt for four hundred years, many of those in slavery. God judged the Egyptians with Ten Plagues, and the Israelites left Egypt with great wealth. Unfortunately, this wealth was eventually used to construct the golden calf, a symbol of idolatry, which was later destroyed by Moses.

For our freedom, then and now, we thank God by keeping our part of the promise: To worship one God, and to live according to the Ten Commandments and the Torah.

Raise the cup of wine in thanksgiving.

This promise made to our ancestors also continues for us, for more than one enemy has arisen to destroy us. In every generation there are those who seek our destruction, but the Holy One, who is to be praised, saves us from their hands.

Replace the cup.

וְהִיא שֶׁעָמְדָה לַאֲבוֹתֵינוּ וְלָנוּ.
שֶׁלֹּא אֶחָד בִּלְבָד, עָמַד עָלֵינוּ לְכַלּוֹתֵנוּ.
אֶלָּא שֶׁבְּכָל דּוֹר וָדוֹר, עוֹמְדִים עָלֵינוּ לְכַלּוֹתֵנוּ.
וְהַקָּדוֹשׁ בָּרוּךְ הוּא מַצִּילֵנוּ מִיָּדָם:

V'hi she'amdah la'avoteinu v'lanu. Shelo echad bil'vad, amad aleinu l'chaloteinu. Ela sheb'chol dor vador, om'dim aleinu l'chaloteinu. V'hakadosh baruch hu matzileinu miyadam.

We've all been "strangers in a strange land."
Given the experience of our ancestors as slaves and as strangers in a strange land (Egypt), the Torah says we should have compassion for others and treat everyone fairly and with respect. Since many families don't live in the lands of their ancestors (making them strangers in a strange land), this commandment is as important today as ever.

God kept the promise; now how about us?
As promised, God delivered our ancestors from Egypt and they left with great wealth. Unfortunately, they turned the wealth into an idol, the golden calf. When Moses destroyed the golden calf, he offered Jews a choice that still stands today: "Those who follow God, come with me." To follow Moses is to reject idolatry and make a conscious choice to follow God's commandments.

The Ten Plagues

As each plague is recited, each of us should pour a drop of wine onto our plate. Even though we celebrate our freedom on Passover, we diminish our full cup of joy by pouring drops of wine to recall the Egyptians' pain during the Ten Plagues and to mourn their loss of life at the Sea of Reeds.

Note: *Some families dip their finger, usually the index or little finger, into their wine cup to remove a drop of wine as each plague is said. Here's why: while Pharaoh's magicians thought they could reproduce the first two plagues, they couldn't reproduce the third plague, lice. After that, they said the plagues must be "the Finger of God." Therefore, using our finger also reminds us that these plagues were not a series of chance events, but the work of God.*

1. Blood   דָּם   *Dam*
The rivers and streams in Egypt turned to blood.

2. Frogs   צְפַרְדֵּעַ   *Tzfardei'a*
Frogs hopped throughout the land of Egypt.

3. Lice   כִּנִּים   *Kinim*
Bugs crawled over the Egyptians day and night.

4. Wild beasts   עָרוֹב   *Arov*
Wild beasts swarmed Egyptian living areas.
(Note: some interpret *Arov* as flies or insects)

5. Cattle plague   דֶּבֶר   *Dever*
Cattle died, leaving the Egyptians with no meat.

6. Boils   שְׁחִין   *Sh'chin*
Boils on the Egyptians' skin made them itch.

7. Hail   בָּרָד   *Barad*
Hail stones rained on the Egyptians for days.

8. Locusts   אַרְבֶּה   *Arbeh*
Locusts ruined the Egyptians' plants and crops.

9. Darkness   חֹשֶׁךְ   *Choshech*
Days of complete darkness covered Egypt.

10. Death of the first born
מַכַּת בְּכוֹרוֹת   *Makat b'chorot*
The first-born Egyptians died.

Were the plagues a series of natural events?
Many have tried to prove that the Ten Plagues were simply an extraordinary coincidence of natural events. While this could explain some of the plagues, it would be impossible to explain away all of them, especially the tenth plague. At first, Pharaoh didn't believe in God. But after all ten plagues, even Pharaoh believed in God and freed the slaves.

The Mezuzah — today's lamb's blood.
The Israelites spread lamb's blood on doorposts to mark their homes so the tenth plague would pass over them. Similarly, the mezuzah (which means "doorpost") marks our houses today as Jews devoted to the ideals of one God, and reminds us of God's commandments and watchful presence. Inside each mezuzah is a scroll with the Sh'ma: "Hear, Oh Israel: Adonai our God, Adonai is One."

Dayeinu

It would have been enough for us.

God has performed so many acts of kindness for us!

Had God brought us out of Egypt, but not punished the Egyptians, *it would have been enough for us.*

Had God punished the Egyptians, but not destroyed their gods, *it would have been enough for us.*

Had God destroyed their gods, but not divided the sea for us, *it would have been enough for us.*

Had God divided the sea for us, but not led us across on dry land, *it would have been enough for us.*

Had God led us across on dry land, but not taken care of us for forty years in the desert, *it would have been enough for us.*

Had God taken care of us for forty years in the desert, but not fed us manna, *it would have been enough for us.*

Had God fed us manna, but not given us the Shabbat, *it would have been enough for us.*

Had God given us the Shabbat, but not brought us to Mount Sinai, *it would have been enough for us.*

Had God brought us to Mount Sinai, but not given us the Torah, *it would have been enough for us.*

Had God given us the Torah, but not led us into the Land of Israel, *it would have been enough for us.*

Had God led us into the Land of Israel, but not built the Temple for us, *it would have been enough for us.*

We are so thankful for the many great deeds that God has performed for us, having: brought us out of Egypt, punished the Egyptians, destroyed their gods, divided the sea for us, led us across on dry land, taken care of us for forty years in the desert, fed us manna, given us the Shabbat, brought us to Mount Sinai, given us the Torah, led us into the Land of Israel, and built the Temple for us to atone for all of our sins.

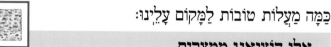

כַּמָּה מַעֲלוֹת טוֹבוֹת לַמָּקוֹם עָלֵינוּ:

אִלּוּ הוֹצִיאָנוּ מִמִּצְרַיִם,

Ilu hotzi'anu mimitzrayim,

דַּיֵּנוּ: וְלֹא עָשָׂה בָהֶם שְׁפָטִים,

אִלּוּ עָשָׂה בָהֶם שְׁפָטִים,

דַּיֵּנוּ: וְלֹא עָשָׂה בֵאלֹהֵיהֶם,

אִלּוּ עָשָׂה בֵאלֹהֵיהֶם,

דַּיֵּנוּ: וְלֹא קָרַע לָנוּ אֶת־הַיָּם,

אִלּוּ קָרַע לָנוּ אֶת־הַיָּם,

דַּיֵּנוּ: וְלֹא הֶעֱבִירָנוּ בְתוֹכוֹ בֶּחָרָבָה,

אִלּוּ הֶעֱבִירָנוּ בְתוֹכוֹ בֶּחָרָבָה,

דַּיֵּנוּ: וְלֹא סִפֵּק צָרְכֵּנוּ בַּמִּדְבָּר אַרְבָּעִים שָׁנָה,

אִלּוּ סִפֵּק צָרְכֵּנוּ בַּמִּדְבָּר אַרְבָּעִים שָׁנָה,

דַּיֵּנוּ: וְלֹא הֶאֱכִילָנוּ אֶת־הַמָּן,

אִלּוּ הֶאֱכִילָנוּ אֶת־הַמָּן,

דַּיֵּנוּ: וְלֹא נָתַן לָנוּ אֶת־הַשַּׁבָּת,

אִלּוּ נָתַן לָנוּ אֶת־הַשַּׁבָּת,

Ilu natan lanu et-hashabat,

דַּיֵּנוּ: וְלֹא קֵרְבָנוּ לִפְנֵי הַר סִינַי,

אִלּוּ קֵרְבָנוּ לִפְנֵי הַר סִינַי,

דַּיֵּנוּ: וְלֹא נָתַן לָנוּ אֶת־הַתּוֹרָה,

אִלּוּ נָתַן לָנוּ אֶת־הַתּוֹרָה,

Ilu natan lanu et-hatorah,

דַּיֵּנוּ: וְלֹא הִכְנִיסָנוּ לְאֶרֶץ יִשְׂרָאֵל,

אִלּוּ הִכְנִיסָנוּ לְאֶרֶץ יִשְׂרָאֵל,

דַּיֵּנוּ: וְלֹא בָנָה לָנוּ אֶת־בֵּית הַבְּחִירָה,

עַל אַחַת כַּמָּה וְכַמָּה טוֹבָה כְפוּלָה וּמְכֻפֶּלֶת לַמָּקוֹם עָלֵינוּ: שֶׁהוֹצִיאָנוּ מִמִּצְרַיִם, וְעָשָׂה בָהֶם שְׁפָטִים, וְעָשָׂה בֵאלֹהֵיהֶם, וְקָרַע לָנוּ אֶת־הַיָּם, וְהֶעֱבִירָנוּ בְתוֹכוֹ בֶּחָרָבָה, וְסִפֵּק צָרְכֵּנוּ בַּמִּדְבָּר אַרְבָּעִים שָׁנָה, וְהֶאֱכִילָנוּ אֶת־הַמָּן, וְנָתַן לָנוּ אֶת־הַשַּׁבָּת, וְקֵרְבָנוּ לִפְנֵי הַר סִינַי, וְנָתַן לָנוּ אֶת־הַתּוֹרָה, וְהִכְנִיסָנוּ לְאֶרֶץ יִשְׂרָאֵל, וּבָנָה לָנוּ אֶת־בֵּית הַבְּחִירָה, לְכַפֵּר עַל־כָּל־עֲוֹנוֹתֵינוּ:

Rabban Gamliel's Seder Obligation

 רַבָּן גַּמְלִיאֵל

Rabban Gamliel used to say: "Those who have not explained these three symbols during the Passover Seder have not fulfilled their duty." The three symbols are:

Pesach — The Passover Offering
Matzah — The Unleavened Bread
Maror — The Bitter Herb

Pesach: The *Pesach* offering that our ancestors ate at their Seders during the time of the Temple — what was the reason for it? To remind ourselves that the Holy One, who is to be praised, passed over the Israelite houses in Egypt. As it is written in the Torah, "You shall say, 'It is the *Pesach* offering for Adonai, who passed over the houses of the children of Israel in Egypt and saved our homes when the Egyptians were struck'" (Exodus 12:27).

רַבָּן גַּמְלִיאֵל הָיָה אוֹמֵר: כָּל שֶׁלֹּא אָמַר שְׁלֹשָׁה דְבָרִים אֵלּוּ בַּפֶּסַח, לֹא יָצָא יְדֵי חוֹבָתוֹ, וְאֵלּוּ הֵן:

פֶּסַח. מַצָּה. וּמָרוֹר:

 (Point to the middle matzah.)

Matzah: This *matzah* we eat — what is the reason for it? To remind ourselves that before the dough of our ancestors in Egypt had time to rise and become leavened, the Holy One, who is to be praised, was revealed to them and redeemed them. As it is written in the Torah: "And they baked unleavened cakes (matzot) from the dough they brought out from Egypt. It did not become leavened, for they were driven out of Egypt and could not delay, nor had they prepared other provisions for themselves" (Exodus 12:39).

(Point to the maror on the Seder plate.)

Maror: This *maror* — why do we eat it? To remind ourselves that, as it is written in the Torah, the Egyptians "made our ancestors' lives bitter with hard labor, with mortar and bricks, and with all manner of labor in the field, and made them slave rigorously in all their labor" (Exodus 1:14).

Who was Rabban Gamliel?
Rabban Gamliel the Elder was a grandson of Hillel, one of Judaism's leading sages (also known for the Hillel Sandwich). Rabban Gamliel lived at a time when Jews were being persecuted, just prior to the destruction of the Second Temple in 70 C.E. He authored many reforms for improving society, including regulations to protect the rights of women.

Why do we no longer have religious sacrifices?
a) They're soooo messy.
b) They began to run out of animals.
c) The animal rights groups complained.
d) The Second Temple in Jerusalem was destroyed.

In Every Generation

בְּכָל־דּוֹר וָדוֹר

In every generation, each person should feel as though he or she had actually been freed from Egypt. As it is written in the Torah, "You shall tell your children on that day, saying, 'It is because of what God did for me when I went out from Egypt' " (Exodus 13:8).

בְּכָל־דּוֹר וָדוֹר חַיָּב אָדָם לִרְאוֹת אֶת־עַצְמוֹ,
כְּאִלּוּ הוּא יָצָא מִמִּצְרַיִם, שֶׁנֶּאֱמַר:
וְהִגַּדְתָּ לְבִנְךָ בַּיּוֹם הַהוּא לֵאמֹר:
בַּעֲבוּר זֶה עָשָׂה יְיָ לִי, בְּצֵאתִי מִמִּצְרָיִם. לֹא
אֶת־אֲבוֹתֵינוּ בִּלְבָד, גָּאַל הַקָּדוֹשׁ בָּרוּךְ הוּא,
אֶלָּא אַף אוֹתָנוּ גָּאַל עִמָּהֶם, שֶׁנֶּאֱמַר:
וְאוֹתָנוּ הוֹצִיא מִשָּׁם, לְמַעַן הָבִיא אֹתָנוּ, לָתֶת לָנוּ
אֶת־הָאָרֶץ אֲשֶׁר נִשְׁבַּע לַאֲבֹתֵינוּ.

The Holy One not only redeemed our ancestors; the Holy One redeemed *us with them*. As it is written in the Torah, "God brought us out from there, so that God might bring us to the land promised to our ancestors" (Deuteronomy 6:23).

Lift the cup of wine and say:
Therefore, it is our duty to thank and praise, in song and prayer, to glorify and honor the One who performed all of these miracles for our ancestors and for us. God brought us:
   from slavery to freedom
      from sorrow to joy
         from mourning to celebration
            from darkness to great light
               from enslavement to redemption.
Therefore, let us sing a new song before God.
                              Halleluyah!

לְפִיכָךְ אֲנַחְנוּ חַיָּבִים לְהוֹדוֹת, לְהַלֵּל, לְשַׁבֵּחַ,
לְפָאֵר, לְרוֹמֵם, לְהַדֵּר, לְבָרֵךְ, לְעַלֵּה וּלְקַלֵּס,
לְמִי שֶׁעָשָׂה לַאֲבוֹתֵינוּ וְלָנוּ אֶת־כָּל־הַנִּסִּים הָאֵלּוּ.
הוֹצִיאָנוּ מֵעַבְדוּת לְחֵרוּת,
מִיָּגוֹן לְשִׂמְחָה, וּמֵאֵבֶל לְיוֹם טוֹב,
וּמֵאֲפֵלָה לְאוֹר גָּדוֹל, וּמִשִּׁעְבּוּד לִגְאֻלָּה.
וְנֹאמַר לְפָנָיו שִׁירָה חֲדָשָׁה. הַלְלוּיָהּ:

The Second Cup of Wine

כּוֹס שֵׁנִי

The second cup of wine recalls God's promise: "I will deliver you from bondage" (Exodus 6:6).

God kept this promise, freeing our ancestors from slavery.

Lift the cup of wine and recite:
Praised are You, Adonai our God, Ruler of the universe, who creates the fruit of the vine.

בָּרוּךְ אַתָּה יְיָ, אֱלֹהֵינוּ מֶלֶךְ הָעוֹלָם, בּוֹרֵא פְּרִי הַגָּפֶן:

Now, we drink the second cup of wine.

Baruch atah Adonai, Eloheinu Melech ha'olam, borei p'ri hagafen.

Rochtzah (6th step)
Wash Your Hands

Rochtzah is the ritual washing of the hands. While there was no blessing for the previous washing (*Urchatz*, the second step), *Rochtzah* is a religious ritual, so we recite a blessing.

While at the table, pour water from a cup or a pitcher over your hands, and recite:

Praised are You, Adonai our God, Ruler of the universe, who sanctified us with commandments and commanded us regarding the ritual washing of our hands.

בָּרוּךְ אַתָּה יְיָ, אֱלֹהֵינוּ מֶלֶךְ הָעוֹלָם,
אֲשֶׁר קִדְּשָׁנוּ בְּמִצְוֹתָיו וְצִוָּנוּ עַל נְטִילַת יָדָיִם:

Baruch atah Adonai, Eloheinu Melech ha'olam, asher kid'shanu b'mitzvo'tav, v'tzivanu al n'tilat yadayim.

Motzi Matzah (7th step)
Blessings over Matzah

The first blessing is the *Motzi*, in which we thank God for the food we eat. The second blessing relates to the special mitzvah of eating Matzah on Passover.

Lift the three matzot and say:

Praised are You, Adonai our God, Ruler of the universe, who brings forth bread from the earth.

בָּרוּךְ אַתָּה יְיָ, אֱלֹהֵינוּ מֶלֶךְ הָעוֹלָם,
הַמּוֹצִיא לֶחֶם מִן הָאָרֶץ:

Baruch atah Adonai, Eloheinu Melech ha'olam, hamotzi lechem min ha'aretz.

Praised are You, Adonai our God, Ruler of the universe, who sanctified us with commandments and commanded us regarding the eating of matzah.

בָּרוּךְ אַתָּה יְיָ, אֱלֹהֵינוּ מֶלֶךְ הָעוֹלָם,
אֲשֶׁר קִדְּשָׁנוּ בְּמִצְוֹתָיו וְצִוָּנוּ עַל אֲכִילַת מַצָּה:

Baruch atah Adonai, Eloheinu Melech ha'olam, asher kid'shanu b'mitzvo'tav, v'tzivanu al achilat matzah.

Now, we eat the matzah while reclining.

Maror (8th step)
The Bitter Herbs

מָרוֹר

Dip the bitter herbs in charoset and recite:

Praised are You, Adonai our God, Ruler of the universe, who sanctified us with commandments and commanded us regarding the eating of *maror*.

Now, we eat the maror without reclining.

בָּרוּךְ אַתָּה יְיָ, אֱלֹהֵינוּ מֶלֶךְ הָעוֹלָם,
אֲשֶׁר קִדְּשָׁנוּ בְּמִצְוֹתָיו וְצִוָּנוּ עַל אֲכִילַת מָרוֹר:

Baruch atah Adonai, Eloheinu Melech ha'olam, asher kid'shanu b'mitzvo'tav, v'tzivanu al achilat maror.

Korech (9th step)
The Hillel Sandwich
Matzah and Maror Together

כּוֹרֵךְ

Place some maror (bitter herbs) between two pieces of the bottom matzah, and recite:

In remembrance of the Temple, we follow Hillel's custom during its existence. Hillel would make a sandwich of the *Pesach* offering, *matzah* and *maror*, and eat all three together, to fulfill the words of the Torah, "They shall eat it (the *Pesach* offering) with *matzot* and *maror*" (Numbers 9:11).

זֵכֶר לְמִקְדָּשׁ כְּהִלֵּל:
כֵּן עָשָׂה הִלֵּל בִּזְמַן שֶׁבֵּית הַמִּקְדָּשׁ
הָיָה קַיָּם. הָיָה כּוֹרֵךְ פֶּסַח מַצָּה וּמָרוֹר
וְאוֹכֵל בְּיַחַד. לְקַיֵּם מַה שֶׁנֶּאֱמַר:
עַל־מַצּוֹת וּמְרוֹרִים יֹאכְלֻהוּ:

Now, we eat the Hillel Sandwich while reclining.

Life is like a Hillel Sandwich.
Some commentators have compared life to a Hillel Sandwich, with bitter herbs sandwiched between the two matzot of redemption. We all go through tough times, but there are a lot of good times, too.

We eat the Hillel Sandwich because:
a) It tastes great.
b) It's less filling.
c) It's low in fat.
d) It's a reminder of the Temple.

Many of us today, Jews and non-Jews alike, quote Hillel without even knowing it.
The Torah says, "You shall love your neighbor as yourself." Hillel, Judaism's leading sage at the turn of the Common Era, explained this phrase to mean, "Do not unto your fellow men, what is hateful to you." He said, "This is the whole Law (Torah), the rest is commentary. Now, go and learn."

Years later, non-Jewish thinkers adapted this phrase from the Torah and Hillel's explanation to develop the Golden Rule.

Shulchan Orech (10th step)
The Passover Meal

שֻׁלְחָן עוֹרֵךְ

Some families begin the Seder meal with hard-boiled eggs placed in salt water.

Eggs are a symbol of life, and because they are eaten at houses of mourning, they are also a reminder that the joy of our freedom is diminished by the Egyptians' pain during the Ten Plagues and their loss of life at the Sea of Reeds.

Enjoy the meal, but make sure that you're still hungry enough for the Afikoman!

Discussion Questions
Ideally, the Seder meal should be a time for discussion about Passover. Try these questions, or even better, ask some of your own.

- *Why is it important to tell our children about Pesach? What is the most meaningful lesson of Passover we can teach our children?*

- *Why does the Seder encourage us to ask questions? So far, has this Seder led you to question things you hadn't before?*

Tzafun (11th step)
The Afikoman

צָפוּן

After the meal, we eat the *Afikoman* while reclining. Break up the *Afikoman* matzah into small pieces, about half as large as an egg, and pass the *Afikoman* pieces around the table. Everyone must eat the *Afikoman* by midnight, and not eat another thing that night.

Don't forget to get a prize for the Afikoman!
Originally, children stole and hid the *Afikoman*, and the leader would search for it. Today, many families do the opposite — the leader hides the *Afikoman* and the children search for it. Either way, it's a long-standing Passover tradition that children receive a prize for the *Afikoman*.

Don't eat anything tonight after the Afikoman!
The Afikoman symbolizes the Pesach sacrifice, which was eaten at the end of the meal before midnight, since that's when the tenth plague was to occur. Today, we don't eat anything after the Afikoman so its taste remains with us through the rest of the evening. This is another way in which we use our senses to deepen the Passover experience.

How did the tradition of the Afikoman begin?
The Afikoman tradition began centuries ago when the Romans ruled the land of Israel. Greek and Roman banquets ended with a dessert, called Afikoman. On Passover, since you're not supposed to eat anything after the last piece of matzah, it became known as the Afikoman, and the prize was developed to keep children interested through more of the Seder.

31

Barech (12th step)

Birkat Hamazon
Blessings After the Meal

This is a condensed version of the Birkat Hamazon.

With 10 or more present, add the words in parenthesis.

A Song of Ascents. When Adonai brings the exiles back to Zion, it will be like a dream. Our mouths will be filled with laughter and our tongues with joyous song. Then it will be said among the nations, "Adonai has done great things for them." Indeed, Adonai has done great things for us, and we will rejoice. Bring us back, Adonai, like streams returning to the Negev. Those who sow in tears shall reap in joyous song. Though he may weep as he carries his measure of seed, he shall return with glad song, bearing sheaves of grain (Psalm 126).

שִׁיר הַמַּעֲלוֹת בְּשׁוּב יְיָ אֶת שִׁיבַת צִיּוֹן הָיִינוּ כְּחֹלְמִים: אָז יִמָּלֵא שְׂחוֹק פִּינוּ וּלְשׁוֹנֵנוּ רִנָּה אָז יֹאמְרוּ בַגּוֹיִם הִגְדִּיל יְיָ לַעֲשׂוֹת עִם אֵלֶּה: הִגְדִּיל יְיָ לַעֲשׂוֹת עִמָּנוּ הָיִינוּ שְׂמֵחִים: שׁוּבָה יְיָ אֶת שְׁבִיתֵנוּ כַּאֲפִיקִים בַּנֶּגֶב: הַזֹּרְעִים בְּדִמְעָה בְּרִנָּה יִקְצֹרוּ: הָלוֹךְ יֵלֵךְ וּבָכֹה נֹשֵׂא מֶשֶׁךְ הַזָּרַע בֹּא יָבֹא בְרִנָּה נֹשֵׂא אֲלֻמֹּתָיו:

Leader:
Friends, let us give thanks.

Leader:
רַבּוֹתַי נְבָרֵךְ.

Others:
May Adonai be praised, now and forever.

Others:
יְהִי שֵׁם יְיָ מְבֹרָךְ מֵעַתָּה וְעַד עוֹלָם.

Leader:
May Adonai be praised, now and forever.
With your consent, friends, let us praise (our God,) the One whose food we have eaten.

Leader:
יְהִי שֵׁם יְיָ מְבֹרָךְ מֵעַתָּה וְעַד עוֹלָם.
בִּרְשׁוּת רַבּוֹתַי, נְבָרֵךְ (אֱלֹהֵינוּ) שֶׁאָכַלְנוּ מִשֶּׁלּוֹ.

Others:
Praised be (our God,) the One whose food we have eaten and through whose goodness we live.

Others:
בָּרוּךְ (אֱלֹהֵינוּ) שֶׁאָכַלְנוּ מִשֶּׁלּוֹ וּבְטוּבוֹ חָיִינוּ.

Leader:
Praised be (our God), the One whose food we have eaten and through whose goodness we live.

Leader:
בָּרוּךְ (אֱלֹהֵינוּ) שֶׁאָכַלְנוּ מִשֶּׁלּוֹ וּבְטוּבוֹ חָיִינוּ.

Together:
Praised be God and praised be God's name.

Together:
בָּרוּךְ הוּא וּבָרוּךְ שְׁמוֹ:

Praised are You, Adonai our God, Ruler of the universe, who sustains the entire world with kindness and compassion. God provides food for all flesh, for God's lovingkindness endures forever. Through God's great goodness, we have never lacked food; may we never lack sustenance for the sake of God's great name. God sustains all life and is good to all, providing food and sustenance for every creature. Praised are You, Adonai, who sustains all life.

בָּרוּךְ אַתָּה יְיָ, אֱלֹהֵינוּ מֶלֶךְ הָעוֹלָם, הַזָּן אֶת הָעוֹלָם כֻּלּוֹ בְּטוּבוֹ בְּחֵן בְּחֶסֶד וּבְרַחֲמִים הוּא נוֹתֵן לֶחֶם לְכָל בָּשָׂר כִּי לְעוֹלָם חַסְדּוֹ. וּבְטוּבוֹ הַגָּדוֹל תָּמִיד לֹא חָסַר לָנוּ, וְאַל יֶחְסַר לָנוּ מָזוֹן לְעוֹלָם וָעֶד. בַּעֲבוּר שְׁמוֹ הַגָּדוֹל, כִּי הוּא אֵל זָן וּמְפַרְנֵס לַכֹּל וּמֵטִיב לַכֹּל, וּמֵכִין מָזוֹן לְכָל בְּרִיּוֹתָיו אֲשֶׁר בָּרָא. בָּרוּךְ אַתָּה יְיָ, הַזָּן אֶת הַכֹּל:

We thank You, Adonai our God, for giving our ancestors a good, desirable and spacious land, for the covenant and Torah, and for life and sustenance. May Your name be praised forever by all who live. As it is written in the Torah, "When you have eaten and are satisfied, you shall praise Adonai your God for the good land that God has given you." Praised are You, Adonai, for that land and for our sustenance.

נוֹדֶה לְּךָ יְיָ אֱלֹהֵינוּ עַל שֶׁהִנְחַלְתָּ לַאֲבוֹתֵינוּ,
אֶרֶץ חֶמְדָּה טוֹבָה וּרְחָבָה, בְּרִית וְתוֹרָה, חַיִּים
וּמָזוֹן, יִתְבָּרַךְ שִׁמְךָ בְּפִי כָל חַי תָּמִיד לְעוֹלָם וָעֶד.

כַּכָּתוּב, וְאָכַלְתָּ וְשָׂבָעְתָּ, וּבֵרַכְתָּ אֶת יְיָ אֱלֹהֶיךָ
עַל הָאָרֶץ הַטֹּבָה אֲשֶׁר נָתַן לָךְ.
בָּרוּךְ אַתָּה יְיָ, עַל הָאָרֶץ וְעַל הַמָּזוֹן:

Rebuild Jerusalem the holy city, speedily, in our days. Praised are You, Adonai, who in mercy rebuilds Jerusalem. Amen.

וּבְנֵה יְרוּשָׁלַיִם עִיר הַקֹּדֶשׁ בִּמְהֵרָה בְיָמֵינוּ.
בָּרוּךְ אַתָּה יְיָ, בּוֹנֵה בְרַחֲמָיו יְרוּשָׁלָיִם. אָמֵן.

Praised are You, Adonai our God, Ruler of the universe, who does good for us each day and will continue to do good for us. May You continue to treat us with kindness and compassion. And may we be worthy of the days of the Messiah.

בָּרוּךְ אַתָּה יְיָ, אֱלֹהֵינוּ מֶלֶךְ הָעוֹלָם, הַמֶּלֶךְ הַטּוֹב,
וְהַמֵּטִיב לַכֹּל, הוּא הֵטִיב, הוּא מֵטִיב, הוּא
יֵיטִיב לָנוּ, הוּא גְמָלָנוּ, הוּא גוֹמְלֵנוּ, הוּא יִגְמְלֵנוּ
לָעַד, חֵן וָחֶסֶד וְרַחֲמִים, וִיזַכֵּנוּ לִימוֹת הַמָּשִׁיחַ.

May the All-Merciful bless all who are gathered here.

הָרַחֲמָן, הוּא יְבָרֵךְ אֶת כָּל הַמְסֻבִּין כָּאן.

On Shabbat, add this verse:
May the All-Merciful let us inherit the day of true Shabbat rest and rest for eternal life.

On Shabbat, add this verse:
הָרַחֲמָן, הוּא יַנְחִילֵנוּ יוֹם שֶׁכֻּלּוֹ שַׁבָּת
וּמְנוּחָה לְחַיֵּי הָעוֹלָמִים.

May the All-Merciful let us inherit the day that is completely good.

הָרַחֲמָן, הוּא יַנְחִילֵנוּ יוֹם שֶׁכֻּלּוֹ טוֹב.

May the All-Merciful bless the State of Israel, the promise of our redemption.

הָרַחֲמָן, הוּא יְבָרֵךְ אֶת מְדִינַת יִשְׂרָאֵל,
רֵאשִׁית צְמִיחַת גְּאֻלָּתֵנוּ.

God is a tower of salvation and shows lovingkindness to David, the annointed, and to his descendants forevermore. May the One who brings peace to the universe, bring peace to us, and to all Israel. And let us say: Amen.

מִגְדּוֹל יְשׁוּעוֹת מַלְכּוֹ, וְעֹשֶׂה חֶסֶד לִמְשִׁיחוֹ
לְדָוִד וּלְזַרְעוֹ עַד עוֹלָם:
עֹשֶׂה שָׁלוֹם בִּמְרוֹמָיו, הוּא יַעֲשֶׂה שָׁלוֹם,
עָלֵינוּ וְעַל כָּל יִשְׂרָאֵל, וְאִמְרוּ אָמֵן:

May Adonai give strength to our people. May Adonai bless our people with peace.

יְיָ עֹז לְעַמּוֹ יִתֵּן,
יְיָ יְבָרֵךְ אֶת עַמּוֹ בַשָּׁלוֹם:

What was the first source of the Birkat Hamazon?
a) The Mishnah.
b) The Talmud.
c) The Torah.
d) The Beatles.

You too can speak the words of Moses!
Tradition tells us that when manna rained from the sky, Moses said, "Praised are You, Adonai, who sustains all life." We say those words in the Birkat Hamazon: בָּרוּךְ אַתָּה יְיָ, הַזָּן אֶת הַכֹּל
Take a look, it's at the bottom of page 32.

The Third Cup of Wine

כּוֹס שְׁלִישִׁי

The third cup of wine recalls God's promise, "I will redeem you with an outstretched arm, and with great judgments" (Exodus 6:6).

God kept this promise of redemption by freeing us through many miracles with an "outstretched arm," such as the "judgments" of the Ten Plagues and our crossing at the Sea of Reeds.

Lift the wine cup and recite:
Praised are You, Adonai our God, Ruler of the universe, who creates the fruit of the vine.

Now, we drink the third cup of wine.

 בָּרוּךְ אַתָּה יְיָ, אֱלֹהֵינוּ מֶלֶךְ הָעוֹלָם, בּוֹרֵא פְּרִי הַגָּפֶן:

Baruch atah Adonai, Eloheinu Melech ha'olam, borei p'ri hagafen.

Ani Ma'amin
I Believe

אֲנִי מַאֲמִין

Ani Ma'amin is one of the principles of Judaism taught by Rabbi Moses Ben Maimon, better known as Maimonides, who was a leader in the development of Jewish law in the 12th century. The song version of the Hebrew is an important addition to the Passover Seder.

I believe with all my heart
in the coming of the Messiah,
And although he may be delayed,
I will wait every day for his arrival.

 אֲנִי מַאֲמִין בֶּאֱמוּנָה שְׁלֵמָה בְּבִיאַת הַמָּשִׁיחַ, וְאַף עַל פִּי שֶׁיִּתְמַהְמֵהַּ, עִם כָּל-זֶה אֲנִי מַאֲמִין, עִם כָּל-זֶה אֲחַכֶּה-לוֹ בְּכָל-יוֹם שֶׁיָּבוֹא:

Ani ma'amin be'emunah sh'leima, b'vi'at ha'mashiach, v'af al pi she'yitmah'mei'ah, im kol-zeh ani ma'amin, im kol-zeh, achakeh-lo b'chol-yom she'yavo.

Ani Ma'amin is a time to remember those we lost in the Holocaust and other tragedies.
The third cup of wine recalls God's promise to redeem us, freeing us from slavery in Egypt. When we say Ani Ma'amin, we remember those of our people who were not so fortunate and suffered at the hands of others throughout history. Many in the Holocaust sang Ani Ma'amin in their final moments of life to express their faith in God.

Ani Ma'amin during the Holocaust.
These verses were found on a wall in Cologne, Germany, in a cellar where Jews hid from Nazis.

*I believe in the sun,
even when it is not shining.
I believe in love,
even when not feeling it.
I believe in God,
even when He is silent.*

Elijah's Cup

כּוֹס אֵלִיָּהוּ

Open the door to your house, and stand as you sing:

Elijah the Prophet, Elijah the Tishbite,
Elijah from Gilead,
Soon, in our days, may he come together
with the Messiah, the son of David.

אֵלִיָּהוּ הַנָּבִיא, אֵלִיָּהוּ הַתִּשְׁבִּי,
אֵלִיָּהוּ, אֵלִיָּהוּ, אֵלִיָּהוּ הַגִּלְעָדִי,
בִּמְהֵרָה בְיָמֵינוּ יָבֹא אֵלֵינוּ
עִם מָשִׁיחַ בֶּן דָּוִד.

Close the door and be seated.
Keep Elijah's Cup on the table.

Eiliyahu hanavi, Eiliyahu hatishbi,
Eiliyahu, Eiliyahu, Eiliyahu hagiladi.
Bim'heirah b'yameinu, yavo eileinu,
Im Mashiach ben David, im Mashiach ben David.

Kids: Does there seem to be less wine in the cup? Who drank it? Could it have been Elijah?

Could Elijah's Cup be the Fifth Cup?
The tradition of Elijah's Cup may have originated in the Torah, with Exodus 6:8:

> *"And I will bring you into the land."*

In this verse, God looks to our future, with the coming of the Messiah and a lasting peace. Since this follows the verses (Exodus 6:6-7) that have become the basis for drinking the four cups of wine, some call Elijah's Cup, "The Fifth Cup."

Who was Elijah?
Elijah was a great prophet who lived around 900 B.C.E. According to legend, Elijah never died; he rose to heaven in a chariot and vanished. It is said that he will return to announce the Messianic Age, when the world will live in peace and harmony. We open our doors to show that we want Elijah to enter our lives and bring about the Messianic Age.

What will be your contribution to lasting peace?
Too often we open the door for Elijah without truly considering its meaning. While we open the door for Elijah, we also need to open our hearts and minds to help bring about that lasting peace, and take action. Next time you open the door for Elijah, consider opening a door of your own, too.

Hallel (13th step)
Psalms of Praise

הַלֵּל

The Hallel is a collection of Psalms of praise and thanksgiving. This condensed version excludes certain Psalms, which are included in a more traditional Haggadah. We encourage you to read these inspirational verses.

Psalm 115: 12-18

Adonai has been mindful of us and will bless us.
    God will bless the House of Israel.
    God will bless the House of Aaron.
God will bless those who revere Adonai,
    the small and the great.
May Adonai increase you,
    you and your children.
May you be blessed by Adonai,
    The Maker of heaven and earth.
The heavens belong to Adonai,
    but the earth God has given to mortals.
The dead cannot praise Adonai,
    nor those who go down into silence.
But we will praise Adonai, now and forever.
Halleluyah!

יְיָ זְכָרָנוּ יְבָרֵךְ

יְבָרֵךְ אֶת בֵּית יִשְׂרָאֵל   יְבָרֵךְ אֶת בֵּית אַהֲרֹן.
יְבָרֵךְ יִרְאֵי יְיָ   הַקְּטַנִּים עִם הַגְּדֹלִים.
יֹסֵף יְיָ עֲלֵיכֶם   עֲלֵיכֶם וְעַל בְּנֵיכֶם.
בְּרוּכִים אַתֶּם לַיְיָ   עֹשֵׂה שָׁמַיִם וָאָרֶץ.
הַשָּׁמַיִם שָׁמַיִם לַיְיָ   וְהָאָרֶץ נָתַן לִבְנֵי אָדָם.
לֹא הַמֵּתִים יְהַלְלוּ יָהּ   וְלֹא כָּל יֹרְדֵי דוּמָה.
וַאֲנַחְנוּ נְבָרֵךְ יָהּ   מֵעַתָּה וְעַד עוֹלָם,
הַלְלוּיָהּ:

Psalm 117

Praise Adonai, all nations;
    Laud God, all peoples.
For God's love toward us is great;
    And God's faithfulness endures forever.
Halleluyah!

הַלְלוּ אֶת יְיָ, כָּל גּוֹיִם   שַׁבְּחוּהוּ כָּל הָאֻמִּים.
כִּי גָבַר עָלֵינוּ חַסְדּוֹ   וֶאֱמֶת יְיָ לְעוֹלָם.
הַלְלוּיָהּ:

Psalm 118: 1-4

Give thanks to Adonai, for God is good,
    God's kindness endures forever.
Let Israel declare:
    God's kindness endures forever.
Let the House of Aaron declare:
    God's kindness endures forever.
Let those who revere Adonai declare:
    God's kindness endures forever.

הוֹדוּ לַיְיָ כִּי טוֹב   כִּי לְעוֹלָם חַסְדּוֹ:
יֹאמַר נָא יִשְׂרָאֵל   כִּי לְעוֹלָם חַסְדּוֹ:
יֹאמְרוּ נָא בֵית אַהֲרֹן   כִּי לְעוֹלָם חַסְדּוֹ:
יֹאמְרוּ נָא יִרְאֵי יְיָ   כִּי לְעוֹלָם חַסְדּוֹ:

Psalm 118: 21-25

Say each of the following verses twice:

I thank You, for You have answered me;
    You have become my salvation.
The stone rejected by the builders,
    has become the cornerstone.
This is Adonai's doing;
    it is marvelous in our eyes.
This is the day Adonai has made;
    let us rejoice and delight in it.

אוֹדְךָ כִּי עֲנִיתָנִי וַתְּהִי לִי לִישׁוּעָה.
אֶבֶן מָאֲסוּ הַבּוֹנִים הָיְתָה לְרֹאשׁ פִּנָּה.
מֵאֵת יְיָ הָיְתָה זֹּאת הִיא נִפְלָאת בְּעֵינֵינוּ:
זֶה הַיּוֹם עָשָׂה יְיָ נָגִילָה וְנִשְׂמְחָה בוֹ.

Adonai, deliver us!
Adonai, deliver us!
Adonai, prosper us!
Adonai, prosper us!

אָנָּא יְיָ הוֹשִׁיעָה נָּא: אָנָּא יְיָ הוֹשִׁיעָה נָּא:
אָנָּא יְיָ הַצְלִיחָה נָּא: אָנָּא יְיָ הַצְלִיחָה נָּא:

May all Your works praise You, Adonai our God. May the pious ones, the righteous who do Your will, and all Your people, the House of Israel, joyfully thank, praise, adore, exalt, revere, sanctify and affirm Your name, our Ruler. It is good to give thanks to You, and fitting to sing praises unto Your name. From eternity to eternity, You are God. Praised are You, Adonai, Ruler acclaimed with songs of praise.

יְהַלְלוּךָ יְיָ אֱלֹהֵינוּ כָּל מַעֲשֶׂיךָ, וַחֲסִידֶיךָ צַדִּיקִים עוֹשֵׂי רְצוֹנֶךָ, וְכָל עַמְּךָ בֵּית יִשְׂרָאֵל בְּרִנָּה יוֹדוּ וִיבָרְכוּ וִישַׁבְּחוּ וִיפָאֲרוּ וִירוֹמְמוּ וְיַעֲרִיצוּ וְיַקְדִּישׁוּ וְיַמְלִיכוּ אֶת שִׁמְךָ מַלְכֵּנוּ, כִּי לְךָ טוֹב לְהוֹדוֹת וּלְשִׁמְךָ נָאֶה לְזַמֵּר, כִּי מֵעוֹלָם וְעַד עוֹלָם אַתָּה אֵל. בָּרוּךְ אַתָּה יְיָ, מֶלֶךְ מְהֻלָּל בַּתִּשְׁבָּחוֹת.

What does Hallel mean?
(Hint: Halleluyah means "Praise God.")
Hallel means "praise." The Talmud describes two groups of Psalms: 1) Psalms 113-118 are Hallel ha-Mitzri, the Egyptian Hallel; 2) Psalm 136 is Hallel ha-Gadol, the Great Hallel. Both parts of the Hallel are said at the Passover Seder and certain other festivals, although only the Great Hallel is said at regular Shabbat services. The text for the Great Hallel can be found in a more traditional Haggadah.

Hallel: From the Sea of Reeds to the Temple.
*Some believe the Egyptian Hallel, Psalms 113-118, was chanted when the waters parted at the Sea of Reeds and later in the Temple during the Pesach ritual. The Egyptian Hallel begins, "Halleluyah! Praise, you servants of Adonai." Commentators say this opening phrase suggests that **through the Exodus, the Jews were transformed from servants of Pharaoh to servants of God.***

Ki Lo Na'eh, Ki Lo Ya'eh.
*To God, praise is proper,
to God, praise is due.*

כִּי לוֹ נָאֶה, כִּי לוֹ יָאֶה.

This song praises God by emphasizing many of God's qualities, such as being powerful, humble and holy. The qualities are arranged in an alphabetical acrostic, beginning with the Hebrew letter alef א, as noted by the large, bold letters.

Ki lo na'eh, ki lo ya'eh.

כִּי לוֹ נָאֶה, כִּי לוֹ יָאֶה.

*Adir bim'lucha, bachur ka'halacha,
g'dudav yomru lo:*

אַדִּיר בִּמְלוּכָה, בָּחוּר כַּהֲלָכָה, גְּדוּדָיו יֹאמְרוּ לוֹ:

(Refrain)
*L'cha u'l'cha, l'cha ki l'cha,
l'cha af l'cha, l'cha Adonai ha'mam'lacha.
Ki lo na'eh, ki lo ya'eh.*

(Refrain)
לְךָ וּלְךָ, לְךָ כִּי לְךָ,
לְךָ אַף לְךָ, לְךָ יְיָ הַמַּמְלָכָה.
כִּי לוֹ נָאֶה, כִּי לוֹ יָאֶה.

*Dagul bim'lucha, hadur ka'halacha,
vatikav yomru lo:* (Refrain)

דָּגוּל בִּמְלוּכָה, הָדוּר כַּהֲלָכָה, וָתִיקָיו יֹאמְרוּ לוֹ:
(Refrain)

*Zakai bim'lucha, chasin ka'halacha,
tafs'rav yomru lo:* (Refrain)

זַכַּאי בִּמְלוּכָה, חָסִין כַּהֲלָכָה, טַפְסְרָיו יֹאמְרוּ לוֹ:
(Refrain)

*Yachid bim'lucha, kabir ka'halacha,
li'mudav yomru lo:* (Refrain)

יָחִיד בִּמְלוּכָה, כַּבִּיר כַּהֲלָכָה, לִמּוּדָיו יֹאמְרוּ לוֹ:
(Refrain)

*Mosheil bim'lucha, nora ka'halacha,
s'vivav yomru lo:* (Refrain)

מוֹשֵׁל בִּמְלוּכָה, נוֹרָא כַּהֲלָכָה, סְבִיבָיו יֹאמְרוּ לוֹ:
(Refrain)

*Anav bim'lucha, podeh ka'halacha,
tzadikav yomru lo:* (Refrain)

עָנָיו בִּמְלוּכָה, פּוֹדֶה כַּהֲלָכָה, צַדִּיקָיו יֹאמְרוּ לוֹ:
(Refrain)

*Kadosh bim'lucha, rachum ka'halacha,
shin'anav yomru lo:* (Refrain)

קָדוֹשׁ בִּמְלוּכָה, רַחוּם כַּהֲלָכָה, שִׁנְאַנָּיו יֹאמְרוּ לוֹ:
(Refrain)

*Takif bim'lucha, tomeich ka'halacha,
t'mimav yomru lo:* (Refrain)

תַּקִּיף בִּמְלוּכָה, תּוֹמֵךְ כַּהֲלָכָה, תְּמִימָיו יֹאמְרוּ לוֹ:
(Refrain)

Adir Hu
Mighty is God

אַדִּיר הוּא

Adir Hu tells of our hopes that God will rebuild the Temple "speedily, in our days." The first two Temples were built by human hands. According to tradition, the third Temple will be built by the hand of God, ushering in the Messianic Era.

Like the previous song, *Ki Lo Na'eh*, *Adir Hu* is arranged in an alphabetical acrostic, which we note in the larger, bold letters. Both songs begin their acrostic with the Hebrew letter *alef* א for the word *adir* (which means "mighty").

Adir hu,

אַדִּיר הוּא,

(Refrain)
Yivneh veito b'karov,
Bim'heirah, bim'heirah, b'yameinu b'karov.
Eil b'nei, Eil b'nei, b'nei veitcha b'karov.

(Refrain)
יִבְנֶה בֵיתוֹ בְּקָרוֹב,
בִּמְהֵרָה בִּמְהֵרָה, בְּיָמֵינוּ בְּקָרוֹב.
אֵל בְּנֵה, אֵל בְּנֵה, בְּנֵה בֵיתְךָ בְּקָרוֹב.

Bachur hu, gadol hu, dagul hu.
(Refrain)

בָּחוּר הוּא, גָּדוֹל הוּא, דָּגוּל הוּא,
(Refrain)

Hadur hu, vatik hu, zakai hu.
(Refrain)

הָדוּר הוּא, וָתִיק הוּא, זַכַּאי הוּא,
(Refrain)

Chasid hu, tahor hu, yachid hu.
(Refrain)

חָסִיד הוּא, טָהוֹר הוּא, יָחִיד הוּא,
(Refrain)

Kabir hu, lamud hu, melech hu.
(Refrain)

כַּבִּיר הוּא, לָמוּד הוּא, מֶלֶךְ הוּא,
(Refrain)

Nora hu, sagiv hu, izuz hu.
(Refrain)

נוֹרָא הוּא, סַגִּיב הוּא, עִזּוּז הוּא,
(Refrain)

Podeh hu, tzadik hu, kadosh hu.
(Refrain)

פּוֹדֶה הוּא, צַדִּיק הוּא, קָדוֹשׁ הוּא,
(Refrain)

Rachum hu, shaddai hu, takif hu.
(Refrain)

רַחוּם הוּא, שַׁדַּי הוּא, תַּקִּיף הוּא,
(Refrain)

Echad Mi Yodei'a
Who Knows One?

אֶחָד מִי יוֹדֵעַ

This song began to appear in Haggadot during the 16th century. Since the song is popular among children, we substituted "mothers and fathers" for "matriarchs and patriarchs" to facilitate the singing.

Despite the song's fun question and answer format, we should be mindful of its title. This expresses the belief that God is One, which is central to Judaism and was reinforced during the time of Passover.

Who knows one? I know one.
One is our God in heaven and on earth.

Who knows two? I know two.
Two are the tablets of the Covenant. One is our God in heaven and on earth.

Who knows three? I know three.
Three are the fathers. Two are the tablets of the Covenant. One is our God in heaven and on earth.

Who knows four? I know four.
Four are the mothers. Three are the fathers. Two are the tablets of the Covenant. One is our God in heaven and on earth.

Who knows five? I know five.
Five are the books of the Torah. Four are the mothers. Three are the fathers. Two are the tablets of the Covenant. One is our God in heaven and on earth.

Who knows six? I know six.
Six are the sections of the Mishnah. Five are the books of the Torah. Four are the mothers. Three are the fathers. Two are the tablets of the Covenant. One is our God in heaven and on earth.

Who knows seven? I know seven.
Seven are the days of the week. Six are the sections of the Mishnah. Five are the books of the Torah. Four are the mothers. Three are the fathers. Two are the tablets of the Covenant. One is our God in heaven and on earth.

Who knows eight? I know eight.
Eight are the days to circumcision. Seven are the days of the week. Six are the sections of the Mishnah. Five are the books of the Torah. Four are the mothers. Three are the fathers. Two are the tablets of the Covenant. One is our God in heaven and on earth.

אֶחָד מִי יוֹדֵעַ? אֶחָד אֲנִי יוֹדֵעַ: אֶחָד אֱלֹהֵינוּ שֶׁבַּשָּׁמַיִם וּבָאָרֶץ.

שְׁנַיִם מִי יוֹדֵעַ? שְׁנַיִם אֲנִי יוֹדֵעַ: שְׁנֵי לֻחוֹת הַבְּרִית, אֶחָד אֱלֹהֵינוּ שֶׁבַּשָּׁמַיִם וּבָאָרֶץ.

שְׁלֹשָׁה מִי יוֹדֵעַ? שְׁלֹשָׁה אֲנִי יוֹדֵעַ: שְׁלֹשָׁה אָבוֹת, שְׁנֵי לֻחוֹת הַבְּרִית, אֶחָד אֱלֹהֵינוּ שֶׁבַּשָּׁמַיִם וּבָאָרֶץ.

אַרְבַּע מִי יוֹדֵעַ? אַרְבַּע אֲנִי יוֹדֵעַ: אַרְבַּע אִמָּהוֹת, שְׁלֹשָׁה אָבוֹת, שְׁנֵי לֻחוֹת הַבְּרִית, אֶחָד אֱלֹהֵינוּ שֶׁבַּשָּׁמַיִם וּבָאָרֶץ.

חֲמִשָּׁה מִי יוֹדֵעַ? חֲמִשָּׁה אֲנִי יוֹדֵעַ: חֲמִשָּׁה חוּמְשֵׁי תוֹרָה, אַרְבַּע אִמָּהוֹת, שְׁלֹשָׁה אָבוֹת, שְׁנֵי לֻחוֹת הַבְּרִית, אֶחָד אֱלֹהֵינוּ שֶׁבַּשָּׁמַיִם וּבָאָרֶץ.

שִׁשָּׁה מִי יוֹדֵעַ? שִׁשָּׁה אֲנִי יוֹדֵעַ: שִׁשָּׁה סִדְרֵי מִשְׁנָה, חֲמִשָּׁה חוּמְשֵׁי תוֹרָה, אַרְבַּע אִמָּהוֹת, שְׁלֹשָׁה אָבוֹת, שְׁנֵי לֻחוֹת הַבְּרִית, אֶחָד אֱלֹהֵינוּ שֶׁבַּשָּׁמַיִם וּבָאָרֶץ.

שִׁבְעָה מִי יוֹדֵעַ? שִׁבְעָה אֲנִי יוֹדֵעַ: שִׁבְעָה יְמֵי שַׁבַּתָּא, שִׁשָּׁה סִדְרֵי מִשְׁנָה, חֲמִשָּׁה חוּמְשֵׁי תוֹרָה, אַרְבַּע אִמָּהוֹת, שְׁלֹשָׁה אָבוֹת, שְׁנֵי לֻחוֹת הַבְּרִית, אֶחָד אֱלֹהֵינוּ שֶׁבַּשָּׁמַיִם וּבָאָרֶץ.

שְׁמוֹנָה מִי יוֹדֵעַ? שְׁמוֹנָה אֲנִי יוֹדֵעַ: שְׁמוֹנָה יְמֵי מִילָה, שִׁבְעָה יְמֵי שַׁבַּתָּא, שִׁשָּׁה סִדְרֵי מִשְׁנָה, חֲמִשָּׁה חוּמְשֵׁי תוֹרָה, אַרְבַּע אִמָּהוֹת, שְׁלֹשָׁה אָבוֹת, שְׁנֵי לֻחוֹת הַבְּרִית, אֶחָד אֱלֹהֵינוּ שֶׁבַּשָּׁמַיִם וּבָאָרֶץ.

Who knows nine? I know nine.
Nine are the months to childbirth. Eight are the days to circumcision. Seven are the days of the week. Six are the sections of the Mishnah. Five are the books of the Torah. Four are the mothers. Three are the fathers. Two are the tablets of the Covenant. One is our God in heaven and on earth.

Who knows ten? I know ten.
Ten are the Ten Commandments. Nine are the months to childbirth. Eight are the days to circumcision. Seven are the days of the week. Six are the sections of the Mishnah. Five are the books of the Torah. Four are the mothers. Three are the fathers. Two are the tablets of the Covenant. One is our God in heaven and on earth.

Who knows eleven? I know eleven.
Eleven are the stars in Joseph's dream. Ten are the Ten Commandments. Nine are the months to childbirth. Eight are the days to circumcision. Seven are the days of the week. Six are the sections of the Mishnah. Five are the books of the Torah. Four are the mothers. Three are the fathers. Two are the tablets of the Covenant. One is our God in heaven and on earth.

Who knows twelve? I know twelve.
Twelve are the tribes of Israel. Eleven are the stars in Joseph's dream. Ten are the Ten Commandments. Nine are the months to childbirth. Eight are the days to circumcision. Seven are the days of the week. Six are the sections of the Mishnah. Five are the books of the Torah. Four are the mothers. Three are the fathers. Two are the tablets of the Covenant. One is our God in heaven and on earth.

Who knows thirteen? I know thirteen.
Thirteen are the attributes of God. Twelve are the tribes of Israel. Eleven are the stars in Joseph's dream. Ten are the Ten Commandments. Nine are the months to childbirth. Eight are the days to circumcision. Seven are the days of the week. Six are the sections of the Mishnah. Five are the books of the Torah. Four are the mothers. Three are the fathers. Two are the tablets of the Covenant. One is our God in heaven and on earth.

תִּשְׁעָה מִי יוֹדֵעַ? תִּשְׁעָה אֲנִי יוֹדֵעַ: תִּשְׁעָה יַרְחֵי לֵדָה, שְׁמוֹנָה יְמֵי מִילָה, שִׁבְעָה יְמֵי שַׁבַּתָּא, שִׁשָּׁה סִדְרֵי מִשְׁנָה, חֲמִשָּׁה חוּמְשֵׁי תוֹרָה, אַרְבַּע אִמָּהוֹת, שְׁלֹשָׁה אָבוֹת, שְׁנֵי לֻחוֹת הַבְּרִית, אֶחָד אֱלֹהֵינוּ שֶׁבַּשָּׁמַיִם וּבָאָרֶץ.

עֲשָׂרָה מִי יוֹדֵעַ? עֲשָׂרָה אֲנִי יוֹדֵעַ: עֲשָׂרָה דִבְּרַיָּא, תִּשְׁעָה יַרְחֵי לֵדָה, שְׁמוֹנָה יְמֵי מִילָה, שִׁבְעָה יְמֵי שַׁבַּתָּא, שִׁשָּׁה סִדְרֵי מִשְׁנָה, חֲמִשָּׁה חוּמְשֵׁי תוֹרָה, אַרְבַּע אִמָּהוֹת, שְׁלֹשָׁה אָבוֹת, שְׁנֵי לֻחוֹת הַבְּרִית, אֶחָד אֱלֹהֵינוּ שֶׁבַּשָּׁמַיִם וּבָאָרֶץ.

אַחַד עָשָׂר מִי יוֹדֵעַ? אַחַד עָשָׂר אֲנִי יוֹדֵעַ: אַחַד עָשָׂר כּוֹכְבַיָּא, עֲשָׂרָה דִבְּרַיָּא, תִּשְׁעָה יַרְחֵי לֵדָה, שְׁמוֹנָה יְמֵי מִילָה, שִׁבְעָה יְמֵי שַׁבַּתָּא, שִׁשָּׁה סִדְרֵי מִשְׁנָה, חֲמִשָּׁה חוּמְשֵׁי תוֹרָה, אַרְבַּע אִמָּהוֹת, שְׁלֹשָׁה אָבוֹת, שְׁנֵי לֻחוֹת הַבְּרִית, אֶחָד אֱלֹהֵינוּ שֶׁבַּשָּׁמַיִם וּבָאָרֶץ.

שְׁנֵים עָשָׂר מִי יוֹדֵעַ? שְׁנֵים עָשָׂר אֲנִי יוֹדֵעַ: שְׁנֵים עָשָׂר שִׁבְטַיָּא, אַחַד עָשָׂר כּוֹכְבַיָּא, עֲשָׂרָה דִבְּרַיָּא, תִּשְׁעָה יַרְחֵי לֵדָה, שְׁמוֹנָה יְמֵי מִילָה, שִׁבְעָה יְמֵי שַׁבַּתָּא, שִׁשָּׁה סִדְרֵי מִשְׁנָה, חֲמִשָּׁה חוּמְשֵׁי תוֹרָה, אַרְבַּע אִמָּהוֹת, שְׁלֹשָׁה אָבוֹת, שְׁנֵי לֻחוֹת הַבְּרִית, אֶחָד אֱלֹהֵינוּ שֶׁבַּשָּׁמַיִם וּבָאָרֶץ.

שְׁלֹשָׁה עָשָׂר מִי יוֹדֵעַ? שְׁלֹשָׁה עָשָׂר אֲנִי יוֹדֵעַ: שְׁלֹשָׁה עָשָׂר מִדַּיָּא, שְׁנֵים עָשָׂר שִׁבְטַיָּא, אַחַד עָשָׂר כּוֹכְבַיָּא, עֲשָׂרָה דִבְּרַיָּא, תִּשְׁעָה יַרְחֵי לֵדָה, שְׁמוֹנָה יְמֵי מִילָה, שִׁבְעָה יְמֵי שַׁבַּתָּא, שִׁשָּׁה סִדְרֵי מִשְׁנָה, חֲמִשָּׁה חוּמְשֵׁי תוֹרָה, אַרְבַּע אִמָּהוֹת, שְׁלֹשָׁה אָבוֹת, שְׁנֵי לֻחוֹת הַבְּרִית, אֶחָד אֱלֹהֵינוּ שֶׁבַּשָּׁמַיִם וּבָאָרֶץ.

Chad Gadya
One Kid, Just One Kid

חַד גַּדְיָא

There's more to this song than meets the eye!

Chad Gadya was introduced into the Haggadah by German Jews. The song is written in Aramaic — not Hebrew — and is adapted from a popular German ballad first produced in the 12th century.

One kid — Israel, which was acquired by God for two zuzim, the two tablets of the Torah. The two zuzim have also been interpreted to be Moses and Aaron.

Cat — Assyria, which conquered Israel in 721 B.C.E.

Dog — Babylonia, which conquered the southern kingdom of Judah in 586 B.C.E.

Stick — Persia, which replaced Babylonia in 538 B.C.E. as the leading power of the Middle East.

Fire — The Greeks, who conquered the Persians in 334 B.C.E.

Some scholars believe Chad Gadya is really the story of the Jewish people — how our enemies have tried to destroy us, but we continue on. Here is an interpretation of the various characters:

Water — Rome, which invaded Judea in 66 B.C.E.

Ox — Islam, which ruled the land of Israel beginning in the middle of the seventh century.

Shochet (Slaughterer) — The Crusaders, who destroyed the Rhineland Jewish communities in the 11th century.

Angel of Death — The Ottomans, who later occupied the land of Israel.

At the end of the song, God kills the Angel of Death and restores the land of Israel for the Jewish people. This has been realized in our generation with the development of Israel as the Jewish State.

One kid, just one kid.
My father bought for two zuzim,
Chad gadya, chad gadya.

Then came a cat and ate the kid
that my father bought for two zuzim,
Chad gadya, chad gadya.

Then came a dog and bit the cat, that ate the kid,
that my father bought for two zuzim,
Chad gadya, chad gadya.

Then came a stick and beat the dog,
that bit the cat, that ate the kid,
that my father bought for two zuzim,
Chad gadya, chad gadya.

חַד גַּדְיָא, חַד גַּדְיָא
דְּזַבֵּן אַבָּא בִּתְרֵי זוּזֵי, חַד גַּדְיָא, חַד גַּדְיָא.

וְאָתָא שׁוּנְרָא, וְאָכַל לְגַדְיָא, דְּזַבֵּן אַבָּא בִּתְרֵי זוּזֵי,
חַד גַּדְיָא, חַד גַּדְיָא.

וְאָתָא כַלְבָּא, וְנָשַׁךְ לְשׁוּנְרָא, דְּאָכַל לְגַדְיָא, דְּזַבֵּן
אַבָּא בִּתְרֵי זוּזֵי, חַד גַּדְיָא, חַד גַּדְיָא.

וְאָתָא חוּטְרָא, וְהִכָּה לְכַלְבָּא, דְּנָשַׁךְ לְשׁוּנְרָא, דְּאָכַל
לְגַדְיָא, דְּזַבֵּן אַבָּא בִּתְרֵי זוּזֵי, חַד גַּדְיָא, חַד גַּדְיָא.

Then came a fire and burnt the stick,
that beat the dog, that bit the cat, that ate the kid,
that my father bought for two zuzim,
Chad gadya, chad gadya.

Then came water and quenched the fire, that burnt
the stick, that beat the dog, that bit the cat, that ate
the kid, that my father bought for two zuzim,
Chad gadya, chad gadya.

Then came an ox and drank the water,
that quenched the fire, that burnt the stick,
that beat the dog, that bit the cat, that ate the kid,
that my father bought for two zuzim,
Chad gadya, chad gadya.

Then came a shochet and slaughtered the ox,
that drank the water, that quenched the fire, that
burnt the stick, that beat the dog, that bit the cat,
that ate the kid, that my father bought for two
zuzim, *Chad gadya, chad gadya.*

Then came the angel of death, who killed the
shochet, who slaughtered the ox, that drank the
water, that quenched the fire, that burnt the stick,
that beat the dog, that bit the cat, that ate the kid,
that my father bought for two zuzim,
Chad gadya, chad gadya.

Then came the Holy One, who is to be praised, and
destroyed the angel of death, who killed the
shochet, who slaughtered the ox, that drank the
water, that quenched the fire, that burnt the stick,
that beat the dog, that bit the cat, that ate the kid,
that my father bought for two zuzim,
Chad gadya, chad gadya.

וְאָתָא נוּרָא, וְשָׂרַף לְחוּטְרָא, דְּהִכָּה לְכַלְבָּא, דְּנָשַׁךְ לְשׁוּנְרָא, דְּאָכַל לְגַדְיָא, דְּזַבֵּן אַבָּא בִּתְרֵי זוּזֵי, חַד גַּדְיָא, חַד גַּדְיָא.

וְאָתָא מַיָּא, וְכָבָה לְנוּרָא, דְּשָׂרַף לְחוּטְרָא, דְּהִכָּה לְכַלְבָּא, דְּנָשַׁךְ לְשׁוּנְרָא, דְּאָכַל לְגַדְיָא, דְּזַבֵּן אַבָּא בִּתְרֵי זוּזֵי, חַד גַּדְיָא, חַד גַּדְיָא.

וְאָתָא תוֹרָא, וְשָׁתָא לְמַיָּא, דְּכָבָה לְנוּרָא, דְּשָׂרַף לְחוּטְרָא, דְּהִכָּה לְכַלְבָּא, דְּנָשַׁךְ לְשׁוּנְרָא, דְּאָכַל לְגַדְיָא, דְּזַבֵּן אַבָּא בִּתְרֵי זוּזֵי, חַד גַּדְיָא, חַד גַּדְיָא.

וְאָתָא הַשּׁוֹחֵט, וְשָׁחַט לְתוֹרָא, דְּשָׁתָא לְמַיָּא, דְּכָבָה לְנוּרָא, דְּשָׂרַף לְחוּטְרָא, דְּהִכָּה לְכַלְבָּא, דְּנָשַׁךְ לְשׁוּנְרָא, דְּאָכַל לְגַדְיָא, דְּזַבֵּן אַבָּא בִּתְרֵי זוּזֵי, חַד גַּדְיָא, חַד גַּדְיָא.

וְאָתָא מַלְאַךְ הַמָּוֶת, וְשָׁחַט לְשׁוֹחֵט, דְּשָׁחַט לְתוֹרָא, דְּשָׁתָא לְמַיָּא, דְּכָבָה לְנוּרָא, דְּשָׂרַף לְחוּטְרָא, דְּהִכָּה לְכַלְבָּא, דְּנָשַׁךְ לְשׁוּנְרָא, דְּאָכַל לְגַדְיָא, דְּזַבֵּן אַבָּא בִּתְרֵי זוּזֵי, חַד גַּדְיָא, חַד גַּדְיָא.

וְאָתָא הַקָּדוֹשׁ בָּרוּךְ הוּא, וְשָׁחַט לְמַלְאַךְ הַמָּוֶת, דְּשָׁחַט לְשׁוֹחֵט, דְּשָׁחַט לְתוֹרָא, דְּשָׁתָא לְמַיָּא, דְּכָבָה לְנוּרָא, דְּשָׂרַף לְחוּטְרָא, דְּהִכָּה לְכַלְבָּא, דְּנָשַׁךְ לְשׁוּנְרָא, דְּאָכַל לְגַדְיָא, דְּזַבֵּן אַבָּא בִּתְרֵי זוּזֵי, חַד גַּדְיָא, חַד גַּדְיָא.

Counting the Omer

סְפִירַת הָעֹמֶר

This is recited only on the second night of Pesach; the Omer is not counted on the first night.

The *Omer* ritual reminds us that our crops are gifts from God. By counting the fifty days from the second night of Passover through *Shavuot*, the ritual also connects our liberation from Egypt (Passover) with the Revelation at Sinai, when we received the Torah (*Shavuot*).

Traditionally, Passover marked the beginning of the grain harvest. The first crop to ripen was barley. On the second day of Passover, a small measure of the crop — *an omer* — was brought to the Temple as a sacrifice. We count the next 49 days, a period known as the *S'fira*, literally, "the counting." On the fiftieth day, *Shavuot*, they brought the next crop to ripen, wheat, to the Temple as a sacrifice.

Stand and recite:
Praised are You, Adonai our God, Ruler of the universe, who sanctified us with commandments and commanded us regarding the counting of the *Omer*.

בָּרוּךְ אַתָּה יְיָ, אֱלֹהֵינוּ מֶלֶךְ הָעוֹלָם, אֲשֶׁר קִדְּשָׁנוּ בְּמִצְוֹתָיו וְצִוָּנוּ עַל סְפִירַת הָעֹמֶר:

Baruch atah Adonai, Eloheinu Melech ha'olam, asher kid'shanu b'mitzvo'tav v'tzivanu al s'firat ha'omer.

Today is the first day of the *Omer*.

הַיּוֹם יוֹם אֶחָד לָעֹמֶר.

Ha'yom yom echad la'omer.

The Fourth Cup of Wine

כּוֹס רְבִיעִי

The fourth cup of wine recalls God's promise of redemption to the people Israel:

"I will take you to be My people and I will be your God" (Exodus 6:7).

Lift the cup of wine and recite:
Praised are you, Adonai our God, Ruler of the universe, who creates the fruit of the vine.

בָּרוּךְ אַתָּה יְיָ, אֱלֹהֵינוּ מֶלֶךְ הָעוֹלָם, בּוֹרֵא פְּרִי הַגָּפֶן:

Baruch atah Adonai, Eloheinu Melech ha'olam, borei p'ri hagafen.

Now, we drink the fourth cup of wine.

Nirtzah (14th and final step!)
Acceptance

נִרְצָה

Nirtzah means, "our observance is accepted." Since we have fulfilled the Passover ritual by completing the Seder, we now ask God to accept our Seder ritual.

It is a common practice in Judaism to ask for God's acceptance after completing an important ritual, such as a Talmud tractate or a Seder.

The *Pesach* Seder is now completed, according to its laws and customs. Just as we were privileged to conduct this Seder, may we be worthy to do so in the future. Oh Pure One, who dwells on high, establish Your congregation countless in number. Soon, may you lead us, the seed of Your stock, redeemed to Zion in joyous song.

חֲסַל סִדּוּר פֶּסַח כְּהִלְכָתוֹ, כְּכָל מִשְׁפָּטוֹ וְחֻקָּתוֹ.
כַּאֲשֶׁר זָכִינוּ לְסַדֵּר אוֹתוֹ, כֵּן נִזְכֶּה לַעֲשׂוֹתוֹ.
זָךְ שׁוֹכֵן מְעוֹנָה, קוֹמֵם קְהַל עֲדַת מִי מָנָה.
בְּקָרוֹב נַהֵל נִטְעֵי כַנָּה, פְּדוּיִם לְצִיּוֹן בְּרִנָּה.

Next Year in Jerusalem!

Everyone sings:
L'shanah haba'ah bi'rushalayim!

לְשָׁנָה הַבָּאָה בִּירוּשָׁלָיִם:

Hatikvah
The Hope

הַתִּקְוָה

Hatikvah was written in Hebrew as a poem in 1878 by N. H. Imber, and was later adopted as the national anthem of Israel.

כָּל-עוֹד בַּלֵּבָב פְּנִימָה, נֶפֶשׁ יְהוּדִי הוֹמִיָּה.
וּלְפַאֲתֵי מִזְרָח קָדִימָה, עַיִן לְצִיּוֹן צוֹפִיָּה.
עוֹד לֹא אָבְדָה תִּקְוָתֵנוּ, הַתִּקְוָה שְׁנוֹת אַלְפַּיִם.
לִהְיוֹת עַם חָפְשִׁי בְּאַרְצֵנוּ, אֶרֶץ צִיּוֹן וִירוּשָׁלָיִם.

As long as the heart of the Jewish soul beats,
And our eyes look toward the East, to Zion,
Then our hope of two thousand years is not lost,
To be a free people,
In the land of Zion and Jerusalem.

Kol-od baleivav p'nima, nefesh y'hudi homiya
Ul'fa'atei mizrach kadima, a'yin l'tziyon tzofiyah.
Od lo avdah tikvateinu, hatikvah sh'not al'payim
Lih'yot am chofshi b'artzeinu,
Eretz Tziyon Vi'rushalayim.

Answers to Questions

Front cover (inside): **What does *Pesach* really mean?**
a) *The Paschal lamb.*
b) *To pass over.*
c) *Passover.*
Okay, we'll give you "c" as correct. But the best answer might be "a." The Paschal lamb was known as the *Pesach*, which was sacrificed to God and eaten at the end of the festival meal. Today, the *Pesach* is symbolized by the *Afikoman.* Answer "b" is also correct. On the night of the first *Pesach* in Egypt, the tenth plague passed over the Israelite houses, but killed the first-born Egyptians.

Page 2: **To help Jews remember the 14 steps of the Seder, the rabbis:**
d) *Created a clever rhyme.*
Before the printing press was invented, very few Jews had a Haggadah. That's why the rabbis created a rhyme to help people remember the Seder's 14-step order.

Page 4: **According to the rabbis, why was a Paschal lamb sacrificed on Passover?**
d) *Egyptians worshipped the lamb as a god.*
The Torah commands the sacrifice of the Paschal lamb in the observance of Passover. The rabbis explain that since the Paschal lamb was worshipped as a god by the Egyptians, its sacrifice was viewed as a courageous practice. The sacrifice expressed the Israelites' desire to end the worship of idols and dedicate themselves to the worship of the one true God.

Page 9: **When Shabbat is followed by an ordinary day (not a festival, like Passover), why do we recite a blessing over spices and sniff them during Havdalah?**
b) *After Shabbat, we lose our extra soul.*
According to tradition, we gain an "extra soul" on Shabbat. Therefore, during Havdalah, which marks the end of Shabbat, we sniff spices to gain extra energy to handle the demands of the week ahead and compensate for the loss of our extra soul. Why bother with coffee?

Page 11: **Why do we break the middle matzah?**
c) *To create the Afikoman.*
d) *To save the other half for later.*
We break the middle matzah to create the *Afikoman*, keeping the smaller half with the other two matzot. Also, some believe that breaking the middle matzah symbolizes our poverty as slaves in Egypt, since a poor man might possibly save a portion of his food to eat later, just in case he became hungry.

Page 11: **Why do we place the *Afikoman* in a napkin or a bag before it is hidden?**
c) *The Israelites wrapped up their dough.*
As they left Egypt in the Exodus, the Israelites wrapped up their dough to protect it from the desert wind and other elements. It makes sense: Who wants sandy matzah?

Page 12: **Why are there tiny holes in matzah?**
b) *To keep the matzah dough from rising.*
The tiny holes are perforations, which are added to the matzah dough to keep it from rising during the baking process. You can also spy on people through the holes!

Page 12: **What does *chametz* actually mean?**
b) *Sour*
Once the matzah is mixed with water, it must be completely baked within 18 minutes. If not, the matzah will ferment and become leavened like regular bread. The fermentation gives off a sour taste, and thus the name *chametz.*

Page 14: **Translated directly from Hebrew, how many "Questions" are actually in the traditional Haggadah text?**
d) *One*
There's really only one Question: "Why is this night different from all other nights?" In Hebrew, the other four "Questions" are not written in question form; rather, they explain why the night is different. For example, the first "question" could be translated: "On all other nights, we eat either bread or matzah. *On this night, only matzah.*" This Haggadah uses today's more popular question format to stimulate discussion.

Page 15: **Are you a "wicked" child? Take the test!**
If you answered yes to any of those questions, then you might be a "wicked" child, according to the commentators. They view the wicked child as rejecting God, since he doesn't recognize the Exodus and God's miracles in freeing us from Egypt. In fact, since he rejects God's role, the commentators believe the wicked child would not have been taken out of Egypt!

Page 19: **What does *Sh'mot* mean?**
a) *Names*
Sh'mot begins, *"V'eileh sh'mot,"* meaning: "And these are the names." The entire first line reads, "And these are the names of the sons of Israel, who came into Egypt with Jacob."

Page 20: ***Mitzrayim* is the Hebrew word for Egypt. What is the real meaning of *Mitzrayim*?**
b) *A narrow place*
As slaves in Egypt, our ancestors were backed into a corner and forced into work they dreaded. That's why the Hebrew word for Egypt is *Mitzrayim*, a "narrow place."

Page 20: **Today, the burning bush is a symbol of:**
c) *Israel*
Since it burned but was not consumed, the burning bush has come to symbolize Israel and its ability to survive throughout its incredibly difficult and heroic history.

Page 20: When first told by God to help free the Israelites, Moses replied:

a) *"Who me? Why would they listen to me?"*

b) *"What will I say when they ask Your name?"*

The answers are paraphrased, but the meanings are accurate. Incredibly, Moses questioned whether he was suited for the mission! Moses even questioned whether the Israelites would listen to a message from God. That took some guts! Would you question God? If you don't believe it, look it up in the Torah, Exodus 3:11-13!

Page 21: God's power helped Aaron turn a rod into a snake. How did Pharaoh's magicians do it?

a) *No big deal; it's an old Egyptian trick.*

d) *Special snakes.*

Believe it or not, some historians believe it was common for ancient Egyptian magicians to turn a rod into a snake, and "snake charmers" continue to do it even today. But this might not have been magic after all. Even today, it is said that a type of Egyptian cobra, known as the *naja haje*, can become as stiff as a rod when pressure is applied to a certain nerve. Equally amazing, when thrown to the ground, the snake can go from stiff to its typical snake-like movement!

Page 21: When Pharaoh's magicians couldn't reproduce the third plague, lice, what did they think?

a) *Oh boy, are we in trouble!*

b) *The plagues must be the finger of God.*

Again, a little paraphrasing, but the magicians realized what Pharaoh wouldn't yet admit — that they were dealing with the one true God. Today, we remember "the finger of God" statement when we dip our own finger into a wine cup to take out a drop of wine after reciting each plague. The drops are removed to diminish our joy during *Pesach* by remembering the suffering of the Egyptian people during the Ten Plagues and at the Sea of Reeds.

Page 21: After the tenth plague, Pharaoh realized he wasn't a god to be worshipped, and:

d) *Asked Moses and Aaron to bless him.*

Pharaoh was so awestruck at the power of God that he asked Moses and Aaron to bless him. With their blessings, Pharaoh hoped God would treat him favorably!

Page 22: The Exodus is so important to Judaism, it is mentioned in every:

a) *Kiddush.*

c) *Scroll inside tefilin.*

The Exodus is mentioned in every *Kiddush*, whether it's *Pesach* or not. In fact, the Exodus is among the four sections of the Torah included in *tefilin*, which are worn as a sign of faith and devotion to God. In Exodus 13:9, the first reference to *tefilin* in the Torah, God says the lessons of the Exodus are to be, "a sign upon your hand, and for a memorial between your eyes." The *mezuzah* contains the *Sh'ma* prayer. As for the fortune cookies, you never know!

Page 22: Many scholars now believe the Israelites crossed at the Sea of Reeds, not the Red Sea, because the Torah calls the sea *yam suf*, and *suf* refers to:

c) *Reeds, which can't grow in the Red Sea.*

For many years, *yam suf* was mistranslated as the Red Sea. In Hebrew, *yam* is sea and *suf* is literally translated as reeds — that gives us the name Sea of Reeds. A second reason is that the Red Sea is a salt water sea, and reeds can't grow in salt water.

Page 23: Today, the double portion of manna on the sixth day is symbolized by two:

a) *Of the three matzot on Pesach.*

b) *Loaves of challah on Shabbat.*

The double portion of manna is remembered on *Pesach*, and on Shabbat, when we have two loaves of *challah*.

Page 23: Why didn't Moses enter the Promised Land?

b) *He disobeyed God.*

c) *He struck a rock.*

In their journey through the desert, the Israelites complained to Moses that they were thirsty. God told Moses to command a rock to give water. But Moses disobeyed and struck the rock with a stick. Worse yet, he did this in front of the Israelites, which could have reduced their respect for God. For those reasons, God wouldn't let Moses enter the Promised Land along with the rest of the Israelites.

Page 27: Why do we no longer have religious sacrifices?

d) *The Second Temple in Jerusalem was destroyed.*

Until the Second Temple's destruction in 70 C.E., religious sacrifices were an important part of Jewish ritual, including the observance of Passover. But since sacrifices were brought to the Temple, once it was destroyed, the ritual was discontinued. Now we place a roasted bone on our Seder plate to remind us of the Paschal lamb that was sacrificed during Passover.

Page 30: We eat the Hillel Sandwich because:

d) *It's a reminder of the Temple.*

While the Hillel Sandwich may be low in fat, Hillel began the practice of eating the *Pesach* (sacrificed Paschal lamb) with the *matzah* and *maror* to fulfill a commandment of the Torah. We continue to eat the Hillel Sandwich today to fulfill this commandment and as a memory of the Temple. Since we don't have religious sacrifices anymore, we no longer include the Paschal lamb in the Hillel sandwich.

Page 33: What was the first source of the Birkat Hamazon?

c) *The Torah.*

This is one oldie that the Beatles didn't write. The first source for the Birkat Hamazon was Deuteronomy 8:10, which reads: "When you have eaten and are satisfied, you shall praise Adonai your God for the good land which has been given to you." That's just seven verses after a sentence you may have spoken yourself: "Man does not live by bread alone." See, it's all in the Torah!

Bibliography

A Different Night
The Family Participation Haggadah
By Noam Zion and David Dishon
The Shalom Hartman Institute; 1997

B'kol Echad
Edited by Cantor Jeffrey Shiovitz
Youth Commission, United Synagogue of America; 1990

Exploring Exodus
By Nahum M. Sarna
Schocken Books; 1986

Likrat Shabbat
By Rabbi Sidney Greenberg
The Prayer Book Press; 1973, 1997

1001 Questions and Answers on Pesach
By Jeffrey M. Cohen
Jason Aronson, Inc.; 1996

Passover Haggadah
By Rabbi Nathan Goldberg
Ktav Publishing House, Inc.; 1949, 1956, 1963, 1966

Passover Haggadah: The Feast of Freedom
Edited by Rachel Anne Rabinowicz
The Rabbinical Assembly; 1982

Siddur Sim Shalom
The Rabbinical Assembly; 1998
The United Synagogue of Conservative Judaism

The Art of Jewish Living
By Dr. Ron Wolfson
The Federation of Jewish Men's Clubs; 1988

The Pentateuch and Haftorahs
Edited by Dr. J. H. Hertz, C.H.
Soncino Press; 1978

The Haggadah; Art Scroll Series
By Rabbi Joseph Elias
Mesorah Publications, Ltd.; 1977, 1980, 1995

The Jewish Book of Why
By Alfred J. Kolatch
Jonathan David Publishers, Inc.; 1981, 1995

The New Jewish Encyclopedia
Edited by David Bridger
Behrman House, Inc.; 1962

Acknowledgements

This Haggadah is the product of countless people and a series of circumstances and situations that spans decades. Like the Israelites' path through the desert, the journey of this Haggadah has not been a straight line, and I thank God for every twist and turn, as well as the ability to create this work and share it with others. I have loved every moment of this book.

In fact, it would be impossible to thank all of the people who had an influence on the content and direction of this book. So many people read drafts and offered comments. I'm sure they will be surprised to see their suggestions in print.

One of the great joys of this book has been my interaction with several phenomenal rabbis and educators. First and foremost, Rabbi Reuven Frankel had a very significant impact on this Haggadah as an editor. But even more than that, he sparked my Jewish spirit (*ruach*) and inspired an intense reverence for the content. This reverence drove me to push for levels of quality that far exceeded my original expectations.

Rabbi Allan Kensky, the Dean of the Rabbinical School of the Jewish Theological Seminary, was also a tremendous editor and I greatly appreciate his efforts and those of others at the Seminary. Several other rabbis were very generous with their editing and counsel, most especially Rabbi Dr. Martin Cohen, Rabbi Alex Felch and Rabbi Jeffrey Katz.

I would also like to thank all of the writers and commentators before me who created such fascinating content and ideas. The books listed in the bibliography, especially the haggadot, were excellent sources for this haggadah and are highly recommended reading. In addition, I thank the Davka Corporation, which gave me permission to use the Hebrew part of The Complete Haggadah for DavkaWriter. I also thank Leah Sosewitz, the illustrator, who created incredible artwork and was a joy to work with.

Most of all, I would like to thank my family for their love, comfort, support and inspiration. To my wife and children, Mom and Dad (of blessed memory), brother and sister, and generations of family Seder leaders before me: words cannot express your impact on me and this book. One of the most powerful inspirations for creating this book was simply a desire to share a wonderful Seder with my kids. I hope this Haggadah inspires more wonderful Seders for them and other children and their families.